A N G E R

31-DAY DEVOTIONALS FOR LIFE

A Series

DEEPAK REJU
Series Editor

Addictive Habits: Changing for Good, by David R. Dunham
After an Affair: Pursuing Restoration, by Michael Scott Gembola
Anger: Calming Your Heart, by Robert D. Jones
Assurance: Resting in God's Salvation, by William P. Smith
Contentment: Seeing God's Goodness, by Megan Hill
Doubt: Trusting God's Promises, by Elyse Fitzpatrick
Fearing Others: Putting God First, by Zach Schlegel
Grief: Walking with Jesus, by Bob Kellemen
Pornography: Fighting for Purity, by Deepak Reju

ANGER

CALMING
YOUR HEART

ROBERT D. JONES

P U B L I S H I N G

P.O. BOX 817 • PHILLIPSBURG • NEW JERSEY 08865-0817

Printed in the United States of America

Library of Congress Cataloging-in-Publication Data

Names: Jones, Robert D., 1959- author.
Title: Anger : calming your heart / Robert D. Jones.
Description: Phillipsburg : P&R Publishing, 2019. | Series: 31-day devotionals for life | Includes bibliographical references.
Identifiers: LCCN 2018054203| ISBN 9781629954769 (pbk.) | ISBN 9781629954776 (epub) | ISBN 9781629954783 (mobi)
Subjects: LCSH: Anger--Religious aspects--Christianity--Miscellanea. | Anger-- Biblical teaching--Miscellanea. | Devotional exercises.
Classification: LCC BV4627.A5 J663 2019 | DDC 241/.3--dc23
LC record available at https://lccn.loc.gov/2018054203

Contents

Tips for Reading This Devotional   7

Introduction   9

Foundational Helps for Calming Your Heart

Day 1: You're Not Alone   17

Day 2: Start with a Person, Not a Problem   19

Day 3: God's Provision in Jesus, Our High Priest   21

Day 4: Bad News and Good News   23

Day 5: Anger Inside and Outside   25

Day 6: Putting Off and Putting On   27

Righteous Anger in God and Us

Day 7: The Righteous Wrath of Almighty God   31

Day 8: God's Wrath, Christ's Sacrifice, and Our Righteousness   33

Day 9: The Perfectly Angry Man   35

Day 10: Righteous Anger Motivated by God's Word   37

Day 11: Righteous Anger, Augustine, and Your Heart   39

Addressing the Heart of Sinful Anger

Day 12: Shallow Popular Explanations   43

Day 13: Why We Get Angry   45

Day 14: What's Wrong with Our Desires?   47

Day 15: Our Prayers Reveal Our Hearts   49

Day 16: Playing God   51

Day 17: God's Grace, Our Hope   53

Day 18: The Repentance Prayers of an Angry Couple   55

Angry Behavior and Godly Replacements

Day 19: The Spirit, the Flesh, and Revealed Anger   59

Day 20: What Revealed Anger Looks Like   61

Day 21: Concealed Anger and Grudge-Bearing   63

Day 22: Don't Get Mad; Get a Grip!   65

Day 23: Don't Get Mad; Get Patient!   67

Day 24: Don't Get Mad; Get Talking!   69

Day 25: Don't Get Mad; Get Gracious!   71

Day 26: Don't Get Mad; Get Reconciled!   73

Day 27: Don't Get Mad; Get Content!   75

Anger at Yourself, God, and Children

Day 28: Anger at Yourself   79

Day 29: Don't Blame God—It's Blasphemy   81

Day 30: Don't Blame God; Learn to Lament   83

Day 31: A Plea to Parents (and All Who Love Children)   85

Conclusion: Where Should You Go Now and Why?   87

Acknowledgments   93

Notes   95

Suggested Resources for the Fight   101

Tips for Reading This Devotional

EARLY IN OUR marriage, my wife and I lived on the top floor of a town house, in a small one-bedroom apartment. Whenever it rained, leaks in the roof would drip through the ceiling and onto our floors. I remember placing buckets in different parts of the apartment and watching the water slowly drip, one drop at a time. I put large buckets out and thought, *It'll take a while to fill them.* The water built up over time, and often I was surprised at how quickly those buckets filled up, overflowing if I didn't pay close enough attention.

This devotional is just like rain filling up a bucket. It's slow, and it builds over time. Just a few verses every day. Drip. Drip. Drip. Just a few drops of Scripture daily to satiate your parched soul.

We start with Scripture. God's Word is powerful. In fact, it's the most powerful force in the entire universe.[1] It turns the hearts of kings, brings comfort to the lowly, and gives spiritual sight to the blind. It transforms lives and turns them upside down. We know that the Bible is God's very own words, so we read and study it to know God himself.

Our study of Scripture is practical. Theology should change how we live. It's crucial to connect the Word with your struggles. Often, as you read this devotional, you'll see the word *you* because Robert speaks directly to you, the reader. Each reading contains reflection questions and a practical suggestion. You'll get much more from this experience if you answer the questions and do the practical exercises. Don't skip them. Do them for the sake of your own soul.

Our study of Scripture is worshipful. Anger can ruin your life. Fundamentally, any struggle with anger is a worship problem.

You might vent your frustrations at your spouse or friend, or you might give him or her a cold shoulder for days—but either way, the primary issue is not your friend or the injustice that you feel. Anger is first a problem with God. It's all too easy to sit as judge of the wrong and to take God's place as the ultimate judge. "I was wronged, so I'm going to do something about it." "How dare you treat me this way? I don't deserve this." "You're a fool, and I'm going to let you have it!"

Defeating anger is not a matter of seeking anger management strategies (as helpful as some might be) but one of turning back to God for his help. The Word points us to Christ, who rescues us from our anger and reorients our life. The goal of your time in God's Word should always be worship. There are no quick fixes when it comes to defeating anger. Fighting it will require orienting your entire life to Christ.

If you find this devotional helpful (and I trust that you will!), reread it in different seasons of your life. Work through it this coming month, and then come back to it a year from now, to remind yourself how to do battle with your anger.

This devotional is *not* meant to be a comprehensive guide to fighting anger. Good volumes are already written for that purpose. Buy them and make good use of them. You'll see several resources listed at the end of the book.

That's enough for now. Let's begin.

Deepak Reju

Introduction

WELCOME TO A thirty-one-day journey. Like any trip, it begins with the first step. You have taken that step by opening this book and starting down a daily path of biblical reflection, personal application, and communion with God. For the next month or so, we will discuss one of the most common problems that everyone faces: anger.

What anger problems are you facing right now? Maybe you argue with your spouse. You frequently disagree, and your fighting sometimes goes nuclear. Sometimes you criticize, speak harshly to, or even belittle your children. Or, rather than the blazing, red-hot kind, yours might be more the icy-cold kind of anger. You might give your coworker or best friend the cold shoulder for a day or a week—better to ignore, you reason, than to engage. Or you distance yourself from someone in your church, perhaps even resigning one of your ministries.

Anger takes many forms—some of which have specific terms of their own: *displeasure, frustration, annoyance, fury, rage, resentment, wrath,* and so on. Whatever we call it, we all experience it and express it. Anger is arguably the most common problematic emotion that people feel. It is universal—prevalent in every culture and experienced by every generation. No one is isolated from its presence or immune to its poison. It permeates all of us and hurts our most intimate relationships. It's a given part of our fallen human fabric.

But, no matter our situation or the extent of our problem, there is hope. The good news for us is that God has much to say in his Word about anger. From cover to cover, in its narratives and its precepts, the Bible is a book about anger and how to deal with it.

Your Goal: Steady Progress, Not Immediate Elimination

What will make this journey profitable for you? Begin by setting realistic goals. Perhaps God recently convicted you of your sinful anger and you are eager to get rid of it. Don't expect to eradicate all your sinful anger in four weeks and to flawlessly respond with godly replacements every day thereafter. You will quickly be disappointed. Your anger problems did not start in a month and won't be solved in a month.

Instead, focus on the journey itself as you walk with the Lord and as his Spirit teaches you and graces you through his Word. Be grateful for God's amazing grace in Christ—grace that forgives your every angry thought or action and that empowers you to change. Be content to learn where anger comes from, how to go to God with it, how to repent of its underlying beliefs and motives, and how to respond in Christlike ways to the triggers that provoke it. As you learn to depend on the Lord and to practice these biblical skills, you will better handle the constant provocations you face.

What will growing spiritual maturation look like? Suppose that, as a marriage counseling professor, I asked my class what they would think of me if my wife and I had recently had a serious argument and then hadn't spoken to each other for two days. I imagine that the students might want to drop the class. ("Should this guy even teach this course?") But then how might they respond if I told them that my wife and I had had the same kind of severe argument a year ago, and that time we hadn't spoken to each other for two *weeks*? Suddenly the students would perk up and would want to learn how we went from two weeks of not talking to two days.

How might you measure your progressive growth in putting off sinful anger and putting on godly graces?

Look for a decreased *frequency* of angry feelings and expressions. For example, instead of averaging three episodes per week (or per day), you average only one or two.

Look for decreased *intensity* in each expression. For example, instead of punching the wall, you initially clench your fist but then relax it. Instead of upper-decibel shouting, you lower your voice.

Look for a decreased *duration* of angry episodes. For example, instead of stewing for three hours, you go to God more quickly than you used to, and he helps you to get a grip on your anger within thirty minutes.

Look for a decrease in the types of *occasions* that provoke your anger. For example, last month, five triggers provoked your anger: your spouse shared with a friend some embarrassing information about you, your children disobeyed, a church member snubbed you again on Sunday, your boss bypassed you for a promotion, and the highway department did a lane repair during rush hour traffic. But now, as the Lord helps you to grow, you might still have some anger struggles with your wife or that church member, but you find yourself getting less upset when your kids rebel, your boss ignores you, and the orange highway cones appear on the morning you are running late.

Look for change that is both short-term (week to week and month to month) and long-term (from one year to another or one decade to another). By God's grace, what you hope for is *decreasing anger* and *increasing godliness* over the course of your life.

Making the Most of Your Journey

How can you best profit from this book? Let me recommend eight practical steps.

1. Find a workable location where you can be alone with God, your Bible, this book, and either a pen and notepad or a computer. The same place each day is usually best.
2. Plan a regular, daily time to meet with God there—view it as an appointment with your heavenly Father. Investing

ten or fifteen minutes each day will pay huge dividends for you over the course of a month.

3. If you miss a day, relax. Just read the one that you missed. Don't tie your journey to calendar dates, and don't skip a chapter in order to "stay on schedule." The entries generally build on each other, so reading them consecutively is best. Reviewing previous entries might sometimes help. God is in no hurry to rush you through this book.

4. If you already engage in a devotional time of Bible reading, consider putting that on hold so that you can give focused attention to your problem of anger.

5. Begin each session in prayer, asking God to speak to you through his Word and to help you. Consider praying the following verses to the Lord (you can copy them on a 3x5 card and then use that card as your bookmark):

> Open my eyes, that I may behold
> wondrous things out of your law. (Ps. 119:18 ESV)

> Search me, O God, and know my heart!
> Try me and know my thoughts!
> And see if there be any grievous way in me,
> and lead me in the way everlasting! (Ps. 139:23–24 ESV)

6. While the devotions can profit you as they are, reading the verses in your own Bible that come before each day's reading, for context, might increase the benefit you will derive from them.

7. Record your insights, reflections, prayers, and so on in the margins of your book or in a journal, notebook, or computer file so that you can track your progress and review them later.

8. Share with others—friends, church leaders, small group members, and so on—what God is teaching you and how

he is helping you. This will both bless them with gospel truth and reinforce those truths in your own soul. Better yet, invite a friend or mentor to take the journey with you, both for their sake and for yours.

I am delighted to write this devotional guide. As one who wrote a longer book on anger years ago,[1] I have enjoyed reviewing what God's Word teaches and tailoring its truth to fit these devotional reflections. These biblical meditations have challenged and renewed my own soul, as I too fight against this very common problem. I trust that these devotions will be a benefit to your soul, too.

FOUNDATIONAL HELPS FOR CALMING YOUR HEART

DAY 1

You're Not Alone

No temptation has overtaken you except what is common to mankind. And God is faithful; he will not let you be tempted beyond what you can bear. But when you are tempted, he will also provide a way out so that you can endure it. Therefore, my dear friends, flee from idolatry. (1 Cor. 10:13–14)

WE BEGIN OUR thirty-one-day journey with four assurances from God—assurances you need in order to fight against your anger.

1. You will face temptations and trials in this life. People and situations can make life hard and can tempt you toward anger. Don't be surprised at this—God isn't. He knows your struggles.

2. Your struggles are not unique. They are common. You are not alone. The path you now walk has on it the footprints of others. Others before you have been tempted to sinful anger. Scripture records scores of such people—some who succeeded and some who failed. Others around you, even brothers and sisters in your church, are tempted right now. More than thirty-five years of counseling have led me to this statistical conclusion: approximately one out of one people struggle with anger.

Moreover, in your struggle with temptation, you have examples not only in people before you and people around you but also in the God-man above you. Jesus was made like us (see Heb. 2:10–18) and was tempted like us (see Heb. 4:15–16) in every way. Your fully human Savior understands your struggles.

3. These temptations will not be too difficult for you to handle. Your faithful God will not let you be tempted beyond your ability to resist. He will not abandon, leave, or forsake you. As Pastor Warren Wiersbe put it, "When God puts His own people into the furnace, He keeps His eye on the clock and His hand on the

17

thermostat. He knows how long and how much."[1] Of course, this assumes that you are handling life God's way—the way that this book will show you.

4. *God always provides a "way out" amid these trials.* "Good," you might say; "that's exactly what I need. I need a way to get out of this bad marriage or hard job or rising debt or chronic pain or . . ." But notice that God does not promise an escape from the temptation. Rather, he promises to enable you to "endure" it. So what kind of "way out" does God promise? The next verse in today's passage tells us. God promises to help you avoid idolatry—the sinful ways in which you are tempted to respond to the trial (including, for instance, anger). Apart from the Lord's help, these temptations and sinful responses can take you down—all the way down to the point of turning away from the Lord. But as you focus on the Lord and handle your pressures his way, you can learn to live out his method of endurance.

Reflect: Read 1 Corinthians 10:1–14 to see the context of today's verses. Notice the benefits that Israel had—but also the desert temptations they experienced and the ways they succumbed to idolatry (see also Num. 11). Consider the biblical lessons we can learn from the warnings and assurances that God made to ancient Israel, ancient Corinth, and us.

Act: Write 1 Corinthians 10:13–14 on a 3x5 note card. On the other side of it, write, "Temptations to anger will come. God knows about them. But I am not alone—others before me, others around me, and my Savior above me have experienced them. God is faithful. He will enable me to withstand the pressures and to resist sin by trusting and obeying his Word." Carry that card around, memorize it, and recite it when you are tempted.

DAY 2

Start with a Person, Not a Problem

Is anyone among you in trouble? Let them pray.
Is anyone happy? Let them sing songs of praise. (James 5:13)

WHERE SHOULD WE begin our reflections on handling anger? We could start with the varied ways we express our anger— sometimes we vent, and sometimes we stew. We could start with why we get angry—what triggers our anger, and what drives it? Or we could start with the antidote to anger—godly behaviors that should replace it, such as self-control, patience, and forgiveness.

Each of these topics is necessary to address, and we will tackle them all in the coming days. But the best place to begin is with God and his explicit invitation for us to come to him.

In today's verse, James addresses two contrasting categories of human experience: times of trouble and times of happiness. He recognizes that in this fallen world we often face hardship and suffering. Alternatively, we also enjoy happy times—days when life goes well and we experience God's goodness in abundant ways. In these two categories we find "all life's experiences, and each of them in turn can so easily be the occasion of spiritual upset."[1]

What should we do, both when things go well and when they go badly? The apostle's answer is amazingly consistent and remarkably simple: go to God! When you face trouble, go to God in prayer, humbly pleading for his help and petitioning him for relief. When you feel happy, you should go to God as well, but this time singing songs of praise.

James's main point? Whatever our situation, whatever our emotional state, we should go to God. As John Calvin put it, "[James] means that there is no time in which God does not invite us to himself. For afflictions ought to stimulate us to pray;

prosperity supplies us with an occasion to praise God."[2] Negative emotions like anxiety or sadness can't keep you from God; positive emotions like happiness and contentment shouldn't keep you from God. God invites you to come. The third stanza of a famous hymn captures these two opposite experiences: "I need thee every hour, in joy or pain; come quickly and abide, or life is vain."[3] In joy or in pain, go to God.

What does our Bible verse today have to do with your anger? Simply this: *go to God.* Anger easily arises when your circumstances bring suffering or when friends, family, or coworkers mistreat you. But God invites you to talk to him. In the coming days, you will learn much about anger; but for today, commit yourself to praying about your anger and seeking God's help.

Reflect: When you feel anger arising inside, what is your reflex response? Where does your mind go? To whom do you talk, if anyone? As James tells us, we should go to God. Yet too often we don't. We neglect, ignore, or forget him. And yet God persistently invites us to come to him. In addition to our verse for today, reflect on the following five passages from the Psalms and on God's promises to hear you when you turn to him for help: Psalm 40:1; 50:15; 55:16–17; 62:8; 116:1–2.

Act: In a word, pray! Talk to God—today—about your anger. Start by honestly confessing your anger to him. And then humbly ask him for help. "Lord, I can't fight this on my own. I need you." Then share your struggle with a mature Christian friend. Begin the habit of relying on the body of Christ to help you fight against your anger.

DAY 3

God's Provision in Jesus, Our High Priest

Therefore, since we have a great high priest who has ascended into heaven, Jesus the Son of God, let us hold firmly to the faith we profess. For we do not have a high priest who is unable to empathize with our weaknesses, but we have one who has been tempted in every way, just as we are—yet he did not sin. Let us then approach God's throne of grace with confidence, so that we may receive mercy and find grace to help us in our time of need. (Heb. 4:14–16)

ON DAY 2 we saw that God calls us to go to him, even when we are angry. But how do we turn to God? And what will we receive when we do?

Today's passage provides answers. We go to God through Jesus Christ, the Son of God. As God himself, Jesus has boundless power to help you deal with anger.

This Jesus is our Great High Priest, whom God has appointed as the one mediator between us and him. This High Priest did not enter some human tabernacle but went all the way into God's presence ("passed through the heavens," v. 14 ESV) to offer his one-time, all-sufficient sacrifice for our sins. Even when your anger escalates, you can rest assured that your relationship with God has been forever secured through Jesus's death and resurrection. Furthermore, this Jesus, who was made like us in every way (see Heb. 2:17), has also been tempted like us in every way and can sympathize with us.

Did you notice the double negative in verse 15: "we do not have" and "who is unable"? This construction makes a strong assertion. If you invited me to your home and I told you, "I will be there," you would be reasonably confident that I would come.

But if I said, "There is no way I will not be there," your confidence would soar.

The point is stunning: there is no way Jesus will not empathize with you. He *cannot not* feel your pain. Like us, he knew hunger and fatigue. (Who falls asleep on a small fishing boat during a severe storm?) He faced poverty, homelessness, and deadlines. He experienced misunderstanding, rejection, and betrayal— both from foes and from family and friends.

Yet, even when provoked to anger and sinned against horrifically, Jesus never sinned. He never gave up, never caved in, and never buckled. His sinless sympathy means that he feels your temptations toward anger and can help you resist them.

Today's passage ends with a direct invitation for you to draw near to this Savior-Priest in prayer. What will you find when you do? Two provisions that you daily and desperately need. You will find *mercy*—forgiving grace that will pardon all your angry thoughts and words. And you will find *grace to help* you in your time of need—enabling grace that will help you to strip away angry patterns and put on new, God-pleasing ones.

What are you waiting for? Draw near now.

Reflect: When angry, will you "approach God's throne of grace with confidence," because of Jesus, in your time of need?

Reflect: Hebrews brightly spotlights Christ's high priestly ministry. Explore the other images of Jesus in Hebrews 1:1–4; 2:5–10; and 3:1–6. Bask in his powerful, radiant deity; his sympathetic, made-like-us humanity; and his death, resurrection, and ascension that give you both the forgiving grace and the enabling grace that you need today.

Act: Memorize Hebrews 4:16. When you are tempted toward anger, or after you have blown it, ask the Lord for his forgiving and enabling grace.

DAY 4

Bad News and Good News

"You have heard that it was said to those of old, 'You shall not murder;
and whoever murders will be liable to judgment.' But I say to you that
everyone who is angry with his brother will be liable to judgment;
whoever insults his brother will be liable to the council; and whoever
says, 'You fool!' will be liable to the hell of fire." (Matt. 5:21–22 ESV)

EVERY CULTURE CONDEMNS murder. This is true in our
day, and it was true in Jesus's day. Here Jesus reminds his hearers
of the Old Testament prohibition against murder and of its judicial consequences.

But then Jesus takes it a step further. He likens anger to murder, saying that anger is the moral equivalent of murder. Jesus
undercuts the notion that as long as we don't kill with our hands
we are acceptable to God. If we have angry hearts or speak angry
words, we still incur God's judgment—even if we never strike or
injure someone.

Our Lord's words bring both bad news and good news. The
bad news is that you are guilty. You likely have never killed someone, but that does not make you innocent. When you internally
judge or verbally criticize someone, you are guilty before God of
heart murder.

The good news arises from the larger context of our passage.
Matthew 1–4 provides the needed backdrop. It paints a rich picture of a grace-filled Redeemer for all who repent and follow him.
He is the heir and culmination of God's covenantal promises to
Abraham and David (see 1:1–17); the Savior who saves us from
our sins (see 1:21); Immanuel—God with us—the one who is
himself God and who brings us the fullness of God's presence
(see 1:23); God's Son (see 2:15) who baptizes with the Holy

Spirit and fire and who bears and brings God's Spirit (see 3:11–17); the new Israel who resists Satan's temptation for forty days in the desert in ways that Israel failed to do in their forty years of wandering (see 4:1–11); and the Messiah who brings God's kingdom (see 4:17) and proves his claim to messiahship by doing works that befit the Messiah (see 4:23–24).

In other words, the Lawgiver in 5:21–22, who exposes your sinful anger in all its internal and external forms, is also the Savior who offers redemption from those uncovered sins. Despite the depth of your sin, the Redeemer is big enough to help you deal biblically with your anger. Never let the weight of your exposed sin drive you to forget the Savior you need most.

This means, my brother or sister, that when you get angry in your heart and then go to God to confess that sin, you are going to a God who loves you, who sent his Son to die for you, and who will forgive you and empower you to fight against your anger.

Reflect: When you get angry, do you remember that Jesus is your *Savior* who wants to help you? Do you run to him for help?

Reflect: Review the descriptions of Jesus above, including the verses, as time permits. If you belong to Christ, you should *always* approach your examination of *any* sin (whether it's anger or anything else) with the Redeemer whom these verses describe firmly in mind. Never read the Sermon on the Mount in Matthew 5–7 outside the context of the display of Christ in Matthew 1–4.

Act: Continue to talk to God honestly, through Jesus Christ, about your anger, as we began doing in day 2. To build on this, be sure, as you talk to him going forward, to specifically address your *inward* thoughts and feelings. Journal your prayers of confession before the Lord, and seek his forgiving and enabling grace (recall day 3).

DAY 5

Anger Inside and Outside

Anyone who hates a brother or sister is a murderer, and you know that no murderer has eternal life residing in him. (1 John 3:15)

WE LEARNED ON day 4 that anger is the moral equivalent of murder but that Jesus provides salvation for those whose angry hearts and evil words make them guilty before God.

Here the apostle John reiterates our Lord's teaching. To hate someone, just like being angry at someone, is to murder that person. Merging the words of Jesus and his apostle John, we find *anger* and *hatred* to be synonyms. Like anger, hatred is internal murder, and it too deserves judgment. In both our hatred and our anger, as we will see later, we play God and judge the person we are angry with. We mentally wish for him or her to be removed from our current path—if not from our lives completely.

If we've been supposing that God forbids only outward expressions of anger, Jesus and John set us straight. Any view that ignores the heart—our beliefs and motives, our attitudes and dispositions—falls short of biblical Christianity. People look at the outward appearance; God judges the heart.

Is today's verse saying that if you struggle with anger, or even hatred, you are not a Christian? No. John is not talking about the occasional outcropping of hateful feelings or angry expressions—he knows that none of us are sinless (see 1 John 1:8, 10). Instead he's referring to a settled, persistent, unrepentant, intentional pattern of hatred against a fellow Christian. Such a disposition is contrary to the new birth that God's Spirit has given those who follow Christ. Such a man or woman is a stranger to eternal life.

What about those of us who do belong to Christ and have eternal life? We must own every hateful thought, word, action, or desire as being murderous in God's eyes. We must not minimize, excuse, or rationalize our sin. When we sin, as believers, we are sinning not against some unknown deity but against our own Father—the God who gave us his Son and his Spirit and who loves us fully and forever. In that sense, our sin is relatively worse than the same sin by an unbeliever.

This in turn calls us to rush to Christ for mercy. Listen to the gospel provision that 1 John describes: "If we confess our sins, he is faithful and just and will forgive us our sins and purify us from all unrighteousness. . . . If anybody does sin, we have an advocate with the Father—Jesus Christ, the Righteous One. He is the atoning sacrifice for our sins, and not only for ours but also for the sins of the whole world" (1 John 1:9; 2:1–2).

Reflect: Are you minimizing, excusing, or self-justifying your sinful anger? When you do so, you are living like a murderer who ignores or excuses his conscience in order to commit evil.

Reflect: The apostle John writes to those who he knows are saved in order to assure them. He furnishes evidence to confirm that they really do belong to Christ. Read 1 John 5:13 and consider how "these things" he has written previously in the letter function to provide believers with the assurance that is the letter's overall purpose. Our verse for today, however, suggests that hatred for fellow believers can call into question our claim to eternal life.

Act: Take each of the angry thoughts you feel toward any person or situation—both thoughts you are feeling already and thoughts you expect will arise based on situations you will likely encounter today—and honestly name each one and confess it before the Lord for what it really is: a murderous thought. Receive God's fresh forgiveness and ask him to help you catch yourself more quickly next time.

DAY 6

Putting Off and Putting On

Get rid of all bitterness, rage and anger, brawling and slander, along with every form of malice. Be kind and compassionate to one another, forgiving each other, just as in Christ God forgave you. (Eph. 4:31–32)

CHANGE. WE ALL want it. That's what led you to pick up this book and take our thirty-one-day journey. You want to see your angry patterns changed into godly patterns.

How does change occur in a Christian? One vital biblical strategy is the put-off/put-on principle. God calls us to put off sin and put on righteousness—to get rid of ungodly behavior and replace it with godly alternatives. In today's passage, Paul applies this principle directly to anger.

What strikes us at once is the sheer number of terms that Paul uses in this passage. He ransacks his mental thesaurus and expresses six varieties of anger. That's not to say this is an exhaustive or scientific list, but it reminds us that anger comes in assorted shapes and sizes and involves our thoughts, words, and actions.

The fact that Paul addresses Christians should encourage us. Jesus and his apostles repeatedly addressed anger because they knew that this sin exists even among sincere followers of Jesus. The presence of remaining sin should not cause us to doubt; it should cause us to double down on our efforts to deal with it so that we will please the Savior who purchased us.

What should we do about our anger? Paul states it plainly: get rid of it! Whatever the shade or degree of anger—Paul piles on these terms in order to invoke the depth and breadth of all possible anger—put off all of it. Kill all manifestations of it completely.

What should replace our anger? Kindness, compassion, and forgiveness. Let's plant deeply into our souls this put-off/put-on principle. It's not enough for us to stop being bitter, rageful, and so on. We must concurrently be kind, compassionate, and forgiving. God designed these relational graces to function together.

How can you put off your anger and put on Christlikeness? Begin by praying for whomever you are angry with, dropping any steps of revenge you were contemplating taking, and doing something good for that person instead.

Why? Note how our passage ends: because God in Christ has forgiven you. God's forgiveness—his decision, declaration, and promise not to hold your sins against you because of Jesus—is our chief biblical motive for forgiving others. The argument is irrefutable, the logic airtight: how can you remain bitter, or slander someone, when almighty God—who had a just reason to pour out his wrath on your sins—fully forgave you?

Reflect: Does your anger make you doubt ("I must not be a Christian if I keep sinning in this way")? Let the certainty of Jesus's death for you prompt you to fight against your anger.

Reflect: Read and reflect on Ephesians 4:17–5:2—the broader context for our passage. Since we have been rescued by God's grace (see Eph. 1:1–4:1) from a dark, indulgent, ungodly past (see 4:17–19) and brought into a saving relationship with Jesus Christ (see vv. 20–21), we should put off our old patterns and put on new patterns (see vv. 22–24). A half dozen specific put-off/put-on examples can be found in 4:25–5:2. Understanding this dynamic is foundational to all Christian growth.

Act: Think of any specific recent incidents in which you felt or displayed anger. Then prayerfully ask the Lord what it would have looked like if you had instead displayed kindness, compassion, and forgiveness toward your offender. Repent of any failure in this area and, in light of his grace toward you, ask the Lord to forgive you and to help you respond more graciously.

RIGHTEOUS ANGER
IN GOD AND US

DAY 7

The Righteous Wrath
of Almighty God

*The wrath of God is being revealed from heaven against
all the godlessness and wickedness of people, who suppress
the truth by their wickedness. (Rom. 1:18)*

IN ONE SENSE this book is about you and your anger. But
we must not start there. Why not? Because, in a very real sense,
God—not you, me, or any other person—is the most angry being
in the universe.

More than a dozen different Hebrew words in Scripture refer
to God's anger against evil. When we add up the Old and New
Testament terms, we find several hundred references to God's
anger in the Bible—far more than the anger that is attributed to
all other people put together. "God is a righteous judge, a God
who displays his wrath every day" (Ps. 7:11).

What is God's anger? It is his whole-person response to
evil—his perfect, pure, settled opposition to sin. It is his holy
hatred for everything that violates his character or misses his will.
Every aspect of God's being—his mind, will, affections, feelings,
and actions—revolts against every aspect of iniquity.

Against what or whom does God get angry? Simply put,
against sinners and their sin. As our passage above affirms, God
maintains—in the present tense, even now—righteous wrath
against all forms of wickedness.

In Romans 1:16–17, the apostle announces that God's gospel
is the power of salvation for everyone who believes in Jesus. Verse
18 begins a section (which lasts through verse 32) in which Paul
prosecutes the entire human race for our suppression of God's

truth, our failure to glorify him and give him thanks, and our rebellion, unbelief, and idolatry. Verse 18 starts off this entire section with an announcement of God's wrath being revealed against all ungodliness and unrighteousness of men. Feel today the weight of God's immense anger against our sin. Does it scare you? It should. Remember how often God is wrathful in the Bible. He is against you and your sin. The greatest question in the Bible is how a sinful people can be with a wrathful God. (We will answer this tomorrow.)

As you consider God's wrath, ask him to give you the same response of judgment against, settled opposition to, and holy hatred for every form of sin—including your anger.

Reflect: Read and reflect on Romans 1:18–32 (along with 2:1–3:20, as time permits) in order to help you feel the weight of God's holy hatred of our sin. Note the progression from the general descriptions of sin in verses 18–23 to the examples of more concrete actions in verses 29–30—including our approval of sinful practices by others (verse 32). Lord, have mercy on us!

Reflect: Thankfully, as we will see in day 8, God has provided a way by which he can both maintain his holy wrath against our sin and also forgive our sin and declare us righteous in his sight. God is concurrently both *wrathful* and also the most *loving* being in the universe.

Act: Ruthlessly identify and own before God every known sin that you practice or entertain. Ask him to impress on you his holy hatred for *all* of your sin. Ask him afresh to forgive you and to help you fight against those sins. Plead with his Spirit to impart to you his own whole-person abhorrence of all forms of ungodliness—including and especially your own. Share your struggle with a mature Christian friend.

God's Wrath, Christ's Sacrifice, and Our Righteousness

For all have sinned and fall short of the glory of God, and all are justified freely by his grace through the redemption that came by Christ Jesus. God presented Christ as a sacrifice of atonement, through the shedding of his blood—to be received by faith. He did this to demonstrate his righteousness, because in his forbearance he had left the sins committed beforehand unpunished—he did it to demonstrate his righteousness at the present time, so as to be just and the one who justifies those who have faith in Jesus. (Rom. 3:23–26)

ON DAY 7, we saw the apostle Paul prosecute every human—both Jew and Gentile, you and me—as being guilty before God and deserving of his righteous wrath (see Rom. 1:18–3:20). But this presents a problem: how can God maintain his righteous anger against our sin and yet passionately love us as his people?

His answer: the cross of Jesus! Six observations from Romans 3:23–26 can enlighten us.[1]

First, your sin must be punished. God cannot maintain his justice without rightly punishing the guilty. "The soul who sins shall die" (Ezek. 18:4 ESV).

Second, God required a blood sacrifice for your sin. The old covenant demanded an animal sacrifice to pay for the Israelites' sins. In the new covenant, Christ our substitute became "the Lamb of God, who takes away the sin of the world" (John 1:29).

Third, Christ's death was an atoning sacrifice (what Bible scholars call a "propitiation") that satisfied God's wrath against you by placing it on Christ, your substitute. He died in your place.

As a result, you are now justly "justified"—declared by God to be righteous in his sight.

God did all this ("God presented Christ as a sacrifice of atonement") in order to display his grace ("all are justified . . . by his grace"). He demonstrated his perfect righteousness by giving us the opposite of what we deserved. God's wrath and God's love met in a spectacular way at the cross!

Finally, this righteousness is yours through "faith in Jesus"— through your trust in Jesus Christ alone as your Lord and Savior. "Whoever believes in the Son has eternal life" (John 3:36). What does all this have to do with your anger? Plenty. Gaze on the Christ who graciously took the divine hit that you deserved. Praise him for averting the wrath that you earned. And let the merciful sacrifice of Jesus soften your heart and incline it toward showing mercy to those who offend you. Defeating your anger is not dependent on you; it's dependent on Christ.

Reflect: Are you *grateful* for Christ's death on your behalf? Are you *thankful*? Anger is blinding; it makes you lose sight of Christ's sacrifice and forget about his grace. Make the gospel central in your life again. Through faith, Christ's righteousness is yours. What good news for you!

Reflect: Peter plants several striking statements about Christ's death in his first epistle. Meditate on 1 Peter 1:18–19; 2:24; and 3:18 (and their surrounding contexts) to see how Jesus's substitutionary death for your sins gives you life, hope, righteousness, and joy.

Act: Sing the gospel! Grab a hymnal (or search online) to find some great songs about Christ, the cross, and redemption. You can also ask your pastors or worship leaders for gospel-centered recommendations. I recommend "And Can It Be?," "When I Survey the Wondrous Cross," "Before the Throne of God Above," "Man of Sorrows," and "Rock of Ages."

DAY 9

The Perfectly Angry Man

Then Jesus asked them, "Which is lawful on the Sabbath: to do good or to do evil, to save life or to kill?" But they remained silent. He looked around at them in anger and, deeply distressed at their stubborn hearts, said to the man, "Stretch out your hand." He stretched it out, and his hand was completely restored. (Mark 3:4–5)

HOW OFTEN HAVE you said, or heard someone else say, "Sure, I was angry; but even Jesus got angry!"? Perhaps we find ourselves willing to admit our anger—only to justify it in the very next breath!

How can you determine if your anger is righteous? In today's passage, when the Pharisees opposed our Lord's intention to heal a man on the Sabbath, he looked at them in anger (see v. 5). Let's consider three criteria of anger that is righteous and see how our Lord exemplified each.[1]

Righteous anger *reacts against actual sin*—not against someone inconveniencing you or violating your personal preference. Jesus accurately perceived the Pharisees' sin—their hard hearts and judgmental eyes, their refusal to answer, and their lack of compassion for this suffering man.

Righteous anger *focuses on God* and on his kingdom, rights, and concerns—not on you and your kingdom, rights, and concerns. Righteous anger throbs with kingdom concerns, not selfish concerns.

It is amazing how seldom Jesus got angry, despite the dozens of ways that dozens of people sinned against him. So why did he get angry here? Not because he took personal offense, but because the Pharisees opposed his mission as God's appointed Messiah. Jesus's healing ministry attested to his messianic call (see Mark 2:12). His choice to heal on the Sabbath underscored his lordship over it (see vv. 27–28). God's will, God's name, and God's glory wholly absorbed our Lord.

Righteous anger *expresses itself in godly, self-controlled ways*. It does not scream, rage, or wallow in self-pity. It does not ignore, snub, or withdraw from people. Christlike mourning, joy, and obedience attend it. It also produces godly ministry—it defends the oppressed, seeks justice for victims, rebukes transgressors, and pursues repentance, reconciliation, and restoration.

Notice Jesus's self-control. He kept his head instead of venting rage. He didn't need a time-out to cool off or gain composure. His anger didn't derail him from mercifully healing the crippled man.

What about the last time you experienced so-called righteous anger? Did someone actually sin, or were you merely inconvenienced? Did that person hinder God's agenda or your agenda? Did you display Christlike grace, self-control, and ministry, or did you lose control, pull away, or make matters worse? Be careful that your claims of righteous anger are not willful self-deception.

Reflect: Take a moment to measure your own anger against the three criteria. Is your anger righteous or unrighteous?

Reflect: Read and reflect on Mark 10:13–16 and John 2:13–17, where anger that meets our three criteria appears again. Contrast these displays of anger with 1 Peter 2:21–23, in which Jesus, amid violent persecution, does not demonstrate anger but entrusts himself to his Father. What makes the difference?

Act: When you next feel a surge of anger, ask God to help you assess it using our three criteria. You will likely find (as I do) that very little of your anger is truly godly. Confess your sinful anger to God and seek his forgiving grace and enabling grace.

DAY 10

Righteous Anger Motivated
by God's Word

I remember, LORD, your ancient laws, and I find comfort in them.
Indignation grips me because of the wicked, who have forsaken your law.
Your decrees are the theme of my song wherever I lodge. (Ps. 119:52–54)

How sweet are your words to my taste, sweeter than honey
to my mouth! I gain understanding from your precepts;
therefore I hate every wrong path. (Ps. 119:103–4)

IS YOUR ANGER typically righteous or unrighteous? Or perhaps is it some mixture of the two? Those of us who belong to Christ know that God's Spirit is progressively making us more like Christ. This means that, while most human anger is sinful, righteous anger is more than a theoretical possibility. We have biblical examples of other people, such as the psalmist here, who expressed righteous anger in the face of serious sin.

We rightly hail Psalm 119 as a tribute to God's Word and a testimony of the psalmist's total devotion to knowing and doing that Word. Yet this psalm also spans the spectrum of godly emotions—and even includes a half-dozen articulations of righteous anger that fit our three criteria from day 9.

In verses 52–54, the psalmist experiences indignation toward ungodly people. This is more than a fleeting feeling or a momentary emotion; it grips him. His anger arises not from personal annoyance but from a settled reaction against those who forsake God's law. Nor is this anger all-consuming. The passage sandwiches this expression of righteous anger between comfort and praise, between confidence and song.

In verses 103–4, the psalmist expresses hatred for evil, which is based not on personal preference but on God's Word. At the same time, this hatred coexists with a sweet delight in God's Word. In his righteous anger, the psalmist is not a raging bull; he is a lover of God's truth and a hater of anything that opposes it. We see this similar Bible-centered dynamic in verses 113–15, 127–28, 135–36, 139, 157–59, and 162–64 of this same psalm.

What drives his godly anger? His love for God and his Word. Scripture not only guides his behavior but also forms his emotions. A regular intake of Scripture will fashion how we feel about the good and bad things we experience. God's Word must guide our responses.

So, how do you respond when someone snubs you in a social setting? When she shares with others confidential information that you entrusted to her? When he fails to return your phone call? How "righteous" is your anger? Remember that the psalmist's anger arose because people *ignored God*—not because they ignored him.

May God help you to love our Savior, who "loved righteousness and hated wickedness" (Heb. 1:9), and to love his Word so much that righteous anger will mark you when it's warranted.

Reflect: Where does unrighteous anger show up in your life? How often do you think of it as "righteous" when in fact it is not?

Reflect: In addition to our Lord (recall day 9) and our psalmist today, Moses (see Ex. 32:19–20), Saul (see 1 Sam. 11:1–6), and Jonathan (see 1 Sam. 20:33–34) also meet our three criteria for righteous anger. Record insights that you glean about godly human anger from all five of these examples.

Act: Commit yourself today to letting your emotions be increasingly formed by God's Word. Meditate on and pray over today's verses. Ask God to cultivate in you proper forms of righteous anger.

DAY 11

Righteous Anger, Augustine, and Your Heart

*Do I not hate those who hate you, LORD, and abhor those
who are in rebellion against you? I have nothing but hatred
for them; I count them my enemies. (Ps. 139:21–22)*

WE CONCLUDE OUR three-day meditation on righteous vs.
sinful anger with some help from the fourth-century church
father St. Augustine. Before his conversion, he came to Rome
to launch his career as a teacher of rhetoric. Upon his arrival, he
began to gather students; but he soon became aware of a ploy that
many of them were using to undercut teacher income.

How did Augustine respond? "My heart hated them, though
not with a 'perfect hatred' (Ps. 139:22), for perhaps I hated
them *more because I was to suffer by them than because they did
things utterly unlawful.*"[1] In other words, his anger fell short of the
psalmist's righteous anger because it focused on himself and his
financial loss more than on the righteous laws of God that the
perpetrators were breaking.

Later, however, after his conversion and his growth as a
Christian, Augustine looked back on these offenders with a more
righteous anger. What had changed? His consciousness of God.
Augustine's anger with the offenders became oriented toward
their rejection of God, not of him. "But at that time," Augustine
concludes, "I would rather, *for my own sake*, have disliked them
for being evil than to have liked and wished them good for You."[2]
Augustine confirms what we saw on days 4 and 5—namely,
that anger is ultimately a matter of the heart. Motives matter.

When your spouse offends you, your children disobey you,
your mother-in-law criticizes you, a church member insults you,

or your boss treats you unfairly—note the pronoun *you*, in each of these cases—ask yourself some questions:

- In the midst of your heated emotion, are you consumed with yourself or with your God?
- Whom do you regard as more offended—you or Jesus?
- Are you angry because of what the person did to you or because of what he did to your Savior, who bore these kinds of sins on a bloody cross?
- Does your indignation arise because God's name has been dishonored or because your pride has been injured?

Learn from Augustine: righteous anger arises because of another person's sin against God, not because of your personal hurts or vengeful desires.

Reflect: Christians sometimes stumble over the "hate" language in verses 19–22. Bible scholars call such passages *imprecations*—pleas for God to judge the wicked. Rather than rejecting them as barbaric or anti-Christian, let these Spirit-inspired passages help you in three ways: by giving you sober illustrations of God's intense wrath toward those who reject him (recall day 7), by reminding you of God's saving grace that spares believers from that deserved wrath (recall day 8), and by stirring you to pray for and share the gospel with the lost.

Act: Today's psalm concludes, "Search me, God, and know my heart; test me and know my anxious thoughts. See if there is any offensive way in me, and lead me in the way everlasting" (Ps. 139:23–24). Ask God to search your heart and help you discern whether your anger is about injured pride, personal hurts, vengeful desires, or anything else that revolves around you instead of him. If so, go to your pastor or a wise Christian friend, confess your anger, and ask for help.

ADDRESSING
THE HEART OF
SINFUL ANGER

DAY 12

Shallow Popular Explanations

But each person is tempted when they are dragged away by their own evil desire and enticed. Then, after desire has conceived, it gives birth to sin; and sin, when it is full-grown, gives birth to death. (James 1:14–15)

WHERE DOES SIN come from? In days 9–11, we saw that most of our anger is sinful and that we deceive ourselves when we think otherwise. Our passage today explains why.

The verse leading in to today's passage tells us that we must not blame God (or, by implication, anyone or anything else) for our sin. Instead, we must blame ourselves. Here, James follows that up with an analogy to outline sin's progression. Sin starts with an evil desire. And our desires are not dormant or passive; they actively hook us and drag us away. Once conceived, our sinful desires give birth to evil behavior. (He likely uses the word *sin* to refer specifically to sinful words or actions, not to when sin first enters the process—this entire process is sinful.)

The result? Death. We don't know whether James refers to eternal spiritual death, temporal physical death, or a deathlike experience, such as feeling God's displeasure or suffering sin's consequences. Whichever kind of death he means, it is something that was not part of God's original plan for us, his image-bearers.

Sinful anger, and the death that results, start in our hearts.

In its quest to understand people without the perspective that the Bible provides, our culture offers shallow alternate explanations for anger. Some people blame their past—trauma, parental abuse, dysfunctional family dynamics. Some argue that present hardships make them mad—unmet "emotional needs," other angry people, road construction. Some say that anger arises from physiological factors—fatigue, chemical imbalances in the brain, hormone deficiencies, bodily disabilities. Some point to bad role models—the plethora of angry athletes, actors, and politicians who parade before us. Some root anger in direct satanic activity—possession or oppression by "demons of anger."

The Bible recognizes such suffering and speaks to it with compassion. There is a real devil who lies and deceives. Our outer man is decaying; illnesses and hormonal changes become occasions for sin. People—both past and present—fail us, hurt us, and abuse us. Moreover, the Bible recognizes that these factors can exert enormous impact on us. They tempt and provoke us, making anger easy and self-control difficult.

Yet provocations are not causes. Satan didn't *make* you "bite off" your coworker's head. Your angry dad didn't *cause* your anger. Your physical illness doesn't *make* you mad. Your kids can't *drive* you crazy. Scripture resists the reductionism, determinism, and dehumanization that the above explanations assume. The causation for our anger lies inside us. As divine image-bearers, we are not passive machines but active moral responders who are accountable to God—dynamic choosers and responsible free agents before the living Lord. It is only when we take responsibility for our sin that we have access to the grace and forgiveness of God and to the power of change through His Spirit.

Praise God for Jesus, who saves his people from their sins!

Reflect: Listen carefully to how your culture (including your family and friends) speaks about anger. You will often hear unbiblical excuses, rationalization, and self-deception. They not only lead to blame-shifting but also enslave us. Have *you* bought into a shallow explanation for your anger?

Act: When you are tempted to explain away your own anger in one of the above ways, remember James 1:14–15. Resist the lies and ask God to forgive you and help you.

DAY 13

Why We Get Angry

What causes fights and quarrels among you? Don't they
come from your desires that battle within you? You desire but
do not have, so you kill. You covet but you cannot get what
you want, so you quarrel and fight. (James 4:1–2)

I LOVE JAMES 4. Throughout more than thirty years of pastoral care and counseling, I have probably shared the above two verses with people more often than any other passage. It's my primary go-to text for helping people to deal with anger and conflict.

Why do I find these two verses so useful? For one thing, they address this very common problem of anger and conflict. While the term *anger* does not appear here, we know that murderous words and actions come from anger in our hearts (see Matt. 5:21–22 from day 4). Every one of us deals with these issues—more often than we want to admit.

Moreover, James pinpoints the cause of our anger: it comes from the desires that battle within us.[1] The verb *battle* presents a military image of our desires as an army that is encamped for warfare—as entrenched troops that are fixed and positioned to fight. It is spiritual warfare in the heart—the battle of the flesh versus the Spirit (see Gal. 5:16–26), the battle of sinful desires "which wage war against your soul" (1 Peter 2:11). James does not refer to normal, legitimate desires but to those desires that battle for the lordship of our hearts. I can and should desire that my spouse love me, but I must not demand this or let it control me.

Clearly James's focus on the cause of relational conflict means that he is not a behaviorist or moralist. He gives no simplistic advice such as "Just say no," "Stop it," "Give it to Jesus," "Nail it to the cross," or "Pray it through at the altar." Perhaps someone has given you such simplistic advice. Maybe you tried unsuccessfully to just quit being angry. It didn't work. You can't just switch off your anger.

Why not? Because your sinful words and actions, as we saw yesterday, come from your sinful desires.

Is it possible for us to understand these desires? We said that James gives no behaviorist remedy. But neither does he advance some ancient psychoanalytic theory that roots the cause in inaccessible forces that lurk deeply within some murky region of the soul and are unlockable only by a trained therapist.

Instead, James diagnoses the problem in amazingly simple yet profound terms: you get angry when you don't get what you want. Simple, but far from simplistic.

Let me encourage you this week to try on this insight and see whether it fits your angry surges or lingering bitterness. What lies are you believing? What desires are you craving? In what ways might you believe and demand that the world should revolve around you, that everyone must serve you, and so on?

Reflect: Read and reflect on Proverbs 4:23; Matthew 12:34–35; Matthew 15:19–20; and Galatians 5:16–24. Notice that our behavior—our words, actions, and emotions—comes from our hearts. Moreover, passages such as Hebrews 4:12–13 teach that the heart includes our "thoughts and intentions" (ESV)—our beliefs and motives.

Act: When you feel anger, immediately ask yourself what you are wanting and/or believing. Write down your answers, talk to the Lord about them, and share them with a wise Christian friend who can encourage you and pray for you.

DAY 14

What's Wrong with Our Desires?

What causes fights and quarrels among you? Don't they
come from your desires that battle within you? You desire
but do not have, so you kill. You covet but you cannot
get what you want, so you quarrel and fight. You do not
have because you do not ask God. (James 4:1–2)

WE RETURN TO the first two verses of James 4 in order to
probe more deeply into how our sinful desires produce anger and
conflict. We saw yesterday that we get angry when we don't get
what we want.

There are two ways in which a desire can be sinful. We might
desire a forbidden object, such as an item that belongs to someone
else. The other way in which desires get poisoned occurs when we
want a good object too much. We might call these inordinate or
ruling desires, or demands. Anger emerges when we don't get the
acceptance, affirmation, appreciation, affection, admiration, and
so on, that we strongly desire.

What did James's readers want? While the text doesn't tell us,
we know that it was not a forbidden item, because James holds
out the possibility that God might give them the item if they ask
him. (We will explore this on day 15.) We know that God doesn't
give evil things to his people (see Matt. 7:9–11). Some writers
suggest that James's readers wanted money. This fits our point,
since money is a good thing. It's not money itself but the love of
money that is a root of all sorts of evil (see 1 Tim. 6:10).

How can you determine when a desire for a good thing (like
acceptance or money, not someone else's television) has become
inordinate? When do good desires become bad masters? Three
tests can help you to know.

47

1. Does your desire consume you? Do you find yourself obsessing over the desire? Do you think about it all day? "I sure wish my boss would. . . ." "I sure wish my spouse would. . . "

2. Do you sin in order to get it? Do you manipulate, scheme, or lie? Do you pressure, nag, or "guilt" someone into meeting your demand?

3. Do you sin when you don't get it? Do you pull away from the person who won't give it to you? This explains why people leave their jobs, their churches, and their marriages. Or do you attack the person? This explains why people argue, slander, gossip, and commit violence—including domestic violence.

My wife and I have made progress in dealing with our anger problems by using these tests. We even developed what we call the "Chorus of the Demanding Heart" (watch next year's Grammy awards for my live rendition):

I want what I want when I want it;
And when I want it, it had better be there.

Reflect: Consider this insight: "James encourages us to examine our desires because it is the only way to understand our anger. Desire lies at the base of every angry feeling, word, and action."[1] What desires are connected to your anger? Is there something you want that you are not getting—acceptance, affirmation, appreciation, affection, admiration, or something else?

Act: Use the three tests above to discern whether your desires for good things have been hijacked into becoming inordinate demands and ruling masters. List your inordinate desires in the margin, as an act of confession. Then turn afresh to the Lord for his forgiving and enabling grace.

DAY 15

Our Prayers Reveal Our Hearts

What causes fights and quarrels among you? Don't they come from your desires that battle within you? You desire but do not have, so you kill. You covet but you cannot get what you want, so you quarrel and fight. You do not have because you do not ask God. When you ask, you do not receive, because you ask with wrong motives, that you may spend what you get on your pleasures. (James 4:1–3)

WE RETURN ONCE more to James 4:1–2, and this time we add verse 3. We saw on days 13 and 14 that we get angry when we don't get what we want; that the desires that produce sinful anger often involve wanting good things too much; and that a desire becomes inordinate when it consumes our thinking, when we sin in order to get it, or when we sin because we don't get it.

In verse 3, we turn to examine what we ask for in prayer. While a full practical theology of prayer goes beyond the scope of this book, James reminds us that we must be sure to ask God for good things and that we must do so for godly reasons, not in service of selfish pleasures. What we ask God for, and how we ask for it, will reveal both our godly desires and our ungodly demands.

In *One Day in the Life of Ivan Denisovich*, Alexander Solzhenitsyn illustrates this truth in a powerful prison scene. The title character cynically questions why Alyosha, a Christian, clings to a God who leaves him hungry in prison. Ivan challenges him to ask God to provide food.

Alyosha's response stuns the skeptic: "Ivan Denisovich, you shouldn't pray to get parcels or for extra stew, not for that. Things that man puts a high price on are vile in the eyes of Our Lord. We must pray about things of the spirit—that the Lord Jesus should remove the scum of anger from our hearts."[1]

49

While it would not be wrong for a wrongly imprisoned person to pray for justice, release, and rations, the story makes a potent point: God values the things of the heart—the removal of "the scum of anger"—above physical provisions.

As verse 3 of today's passage affirms, anger comes from selfish motives—our inordinate "pleasures." The sinful heart craves its own kingdom, not God's, and it unfortunately prays accordingly. In other words, our heart demands can subvert even an act that is godly—in fact, arguably the godliest of all: prayer. The very gift and privilege that God has granted us—the invitation for us to come and talk to him—can become the means by which our sinful heart expresses itself.

Do you pray? For what? Expect your inordinate desires to emerge when you do, and plead with God to help you dethrone them.

Reflect: Do your prayers reflect a *godly* heart? In 1 Kings 3:1–15 we see a stirring picture of prayer in which God commends Solomon for what he prays for and doesn't pray for. After praising God for his goodness to him, Solomon asks God not for long life, riches, or revenge against his enemies, but for God's wisdom so he can govern God's people in God-pleasing ways. You will find it fruitful to reflect on this passage in light of James 4:3 (and other prayers in Scripture).

Act: For the next few days, record your honest prayers in a journal in order to examine to what extent they resemble either godly requests or ungodly demands. Share some of them with a pastor or mature Christian friend, and invite him or her to pray with you and for you in your walk with the Lord.

DAY 16

Playing God

Brothers and sisters, do not slander one another. Anyone who speaks against a brother or sister or judges them speaks against the law and judges it. When you judge the law, you are not keeping it, but sitting in judgment on it. There is only one Lawgiver and Judge, the one who is able to save and destroy. But you—who are you to judge your neighbor? (*James 4:11–12*)

TODAY'S PASSAGE REVEALS a piercing, sobering truth about sinful anger: especially when we are expressing that anger against someone by slandering him or her, we are trying to be God.

In one sense, all sin involves playing God. The first sinful act arose from Adam and Eve's desire to be like God (see Gen. 3:1–6). Murder usurps God's right to give and take life. Stealing seizes God's right to distribute wealth as he wills. Sexual sin challenges God's right to determine how we should use our bodies.

What about anger? As a form of judgmentalism—a negative moral judgment against perceived evil—it is usurping God's right to judge.

My anger with you begins when I mentally legislate how you should act:[1]

- You shall not let the sun go down on my phone call, email, or text message, but shall reply today.
- You shall greet me each Sunday the way fellow church members should.
- Above all, you shall love me the way I want to be loved, with all your heart, soul, mind, and strength.

I may or may not inform you of my demands. But if you break my law, I mentally record your violation. I may or may not tell

51

you your offense or reveal my evidence. Either way, I am the star witness and chief prosecutor against you. I am also the judge, bailiff, and executioner. So I pound my gavel, pronounce my verdict, sentence you to my punishment, and carry out my justice.

Of course, you may be oblivious to this, but you nevertheless remain under my wrath.

Each role that I described, of course, belongs to God alone. There is "only one Lawgiver and Judge." He alone is the one "who is able to save and destroy." When I am sinfully angry, I am playing God.

What does repentance look like? Remove the laws that you impose on people. Drop the charges. Cover the person's offenses with the blanket of Christian love. Erase them from your ledger. Lay down your gavel, descend your judicial bench, and remove your black robe. Refuse to punish that person. Instead, love him with Christlike love.

God—the only Lawgiver and Judge—has not resigned his role or deputized you to assume it.

Reflect: In what ways are you acting like God, in your anger? In what ways have you pushed him off his throne so that you can judge your family, friends, coworkers, or fellow church members?

Reflect: How often do you mentally legislate how others should act? In what ways do you silently accuse them, record their violations, prosecute them in your mind, and quickly pronounce judgment?

Act: Identify those you are angry with and immediately repent in prayer before the Lord. Resign your God-playing, entrust whomever you are angry with to him, and begin to love those people with Christlike love.

DAY 17

God's Grace, Our Hope

*But he gives us more grace. That is why Scripture says: "God
opposes the proud but shows favor to the humble."* (James 4:6)

OUR RECENT DEVOTIONALS from James 4 might have left
you in despair. After all, who can face God with hearts that self-
ishly demand what we want when we want it and that play God
by judging others?

Thankfully, we find abundant hope nestled right in the mid-
dle of verses 1–12. James 4 does more than exposing, diagnosing,
and denouncing our evil desires. God gives more grace. He shows
his favor to those who humble themselves.

Contrary to our culture's "anger management" mentality, God's
answer for anger doesn't center on self-help techniques, program-
matic steps, or therapeutic interventions. James's remedy for angry
hearts is not "how-to" methods but "Whom-to" movements. As
David Powlison has observed, "James's solution to interpersonal
conflict is shockingly vertical."[1] We must go to God himself.

When we do, what kind of grace will God give us? On day 3
we saw from Hebrews 4:16 that from his throne of grace, through
Jesus Christ, God provides his sons and daughters with forgiving
grace and enabling grace.

And we need both. We need God's *forgiving grace*—his mercy
in Christ that pardons all our sins (recall 1 John 1:8–2:2 from
day 5). Our anger is pervasively evil, but his forgiveness is more
abundant. His atoning fountain ever flows for us. His blood never
fails, never runs dry, and never loses its value. There is mercy
available even for selfish demanders (see James 4:1–3), spiritual
adulterers (see v. 4), and God's enemies (see v. 4) who will repent.

Please don't refuse this provision. Once you feel the depth of your anger, you need a Savior big enough to forgive big sinners—sinners who sin inwardly with demanding hearts, not just outwardly with critical tongues. Praise God for our great Redeemer.

Yet we also need God's *enabling grace*—the work of his Spirit within us that empowers us to be and do what he wants us to be and do. It is divine grace that will "help us in our time of need" (Heb. 4:16)—grace that is "sufficient" to sustain us in times of weakness (see 2 Cor. 12:9–10). His grace enables us to forgive those who would provoke our anger. It empowers us to progressively uproot our deep patterns of judgmentalism, evil words, and harmful acts. God's Spirit nourishes, guides, and strengthens us even when our hard circumstances continue.

What must you do to receive his forgiveness and his enabling power? Admit before God that your anger is sinful, tell him you are sorry for it, thank Jesus for dying for these sins, ask God to forgive you based on Christ's death, and ask him to help you resist the next temptation that you face.

Christian, humble yourself before the Lord. Any other posture invites God to oppose you.

Reflect: Humility requires repentance—but also faith. When you find yourself judging others in your anger, how much are you consciously trusting Christ and looking to him for help?

Reflect: Time and space prevent us from unpacking more of verses 4–10. But a careful examination of the pictures of repentance in these verses will deepen your understanding of James's call to humble yourself. For fruitful reflection, underline and pray back to God each verb in verses 6–10.

Act: Are you grateful for both God's forgiving and empowering grace? Memorize and recite often Hebrews 4:16 and James 4:6 so they will be lifeline (and lifetime) texts that give you hope in your fight against anger.

The Repentance Prayers
of an Angry Couple

Submit yourselves, then, to God. Resist the devil, and he will flee from you.
Come near to God and he will come near to you. Wash your hands, you
sinners, and purify your hearts, you double-minded. Grieve, mourn and
wail. Change your laughter to mourning and your joy to gloom. Humble
yourselves before the Lord, and he will lift you up. (James 4:7–10)

TODAY WE CONCLUDE our meditations on James 4. Yesterday we saw that God promises grace to those who humble
themselves before him and own their sin. Now let's consider
two model prayers of repentance that flow from James 4:1–12.[1]
They come from a repentant married couple who frequently have
heated fights.

> Jack: Lord, I'd like a wife who will keep a cleaner house, manage
> the kids better, and show romantic interest. But I don't *have* to
> have these things. In Christ, I don't need them—but I often live
> like I do. The desire for these things rules me. That's why I criti-
> cize Jill. That's why I rant and rave.
>
> Father, forgive me. I have been soaking up the world's lies.
> Help me to reject them. I've cooperated with the devil, who is
> driving a wedge between my wife and me. Help me to resist him.
> Above all, I have played God. I've usurped your throne by de-
> manding that my kingdom come and my will be done.
>
> Thank you for the blood of Jesus, your Son, that paid for all
> my sins—both my hotheaded words and my idolatrous desires.
> Thank you for your Spirit, who enables me to love Jill the way
> that Christ loved the church when he gave himself up for her.
> Help me to love Jill with your kind of love.

Jill: Lord, I'd like a husband who is more patient and gentle. I am sure that's what you want Jack to be, too. But that's between you and him. I can't change him. Craving these things has only made me a sour wife. I'd like Jack to change, but I don't need him to change. With your help, I can be a grace-filled, Christlike wife.

Father, I have taken your role as lawgiver, prosecutor, judge, and executioner. I have decreed that Jack must love me the way I want to be loved. I've kept a record of his sins and replayed them in my mind. I've judged him and declared him guilty. And I've imposed my sentence by withdrawing from him and criticizing him. I've dragged my feet when he has asked me to do a better job with the house and kids.

Forgive me, Lord, for my many sins—especially those in my heart. Thank you for sending Jesus to die for me. Help me to rest in his righteousness and to submit my desires to you. Help me to forgive Jack as you have forgiven me. Holy Spirit, help me to be a wife who pleases you and serves my husband.

Reflect: The above prayers and James 4:7 recognize Satan's influential (though not causal) role in our sinful anger. Reflect on Ephesians 6:10–18 and 1 Peter 5:6–9—two other passages that call us to resist the devil. Ephesians 4:26–27 also reminds us that failing to deal swiftly with our anger at someone gives Satan a foothold in that relationship.

Reflect: How much do your prayers look like Jack or Jill's prayers? How might you better reflect repentance in your prayers?

Act: Write out, and pray repeatedly, a model prayer of repentance based on Scripture. Share your prayer with a pastor or wise Christian in your church. Consider also sharing it with someone who has been on the receiving end of your anger.

ANGRY BEHAVIOR AND
GODLY REPLACEMENTS

DAY 19

The Spirit, the Flesh, and Revealed Anger

Walk by the Spirit, and you will not gratify the desires of the flesh.
For the flesh desires what is contrary to the Spirit, and the Spirit
what is contrary to the flesh. They are in conflict with each other.
... The acts of the flesh are obvious: sexual immorality, impurity
and debauchery; idolatry and witchcraft; hatred, discord, jealousy,
fits of rage, selfish ambition, dissensions, factions and envy;
drunkenness, orgies, and the like. (Gal. 5:16–17, 19–21)

TODAY'S PASSAGE DESCRIBES the civil war that rages within every Christian. The flesh—the sinful desires, tendencies, and patterns that remain within believers—actively fights against the Holy Spirit, and the Spirit in turn wars against the flesh. While sin no longer reigns, it remains in us until the Lord returns (see Rom. 6–7; 1 Peter 2:11; 1 John 3:2–3). Paul's battlefield strategy is to walk by the Spirit.

What does the flesh produce when we fail to live by the Spirit? Paul lists fifteen sins plus an etcetera.

Sinful anger behaves in varied ways. The human heart and its behavior are profoundly complex. Scripture resists simplistic typologies—the kind of categorizing we sometimes see in popular psychology approaches.

Yet the Bible does suggest two broad pathways that angry behavior often takes. I find it helpful to think of the anger that we choose to reveal vs. the anger that we choose to conceal.[1] Revealed anger lets others know and feel that it's there. It's like a firestorm. Concealed anger hides itself from others, but the anger itself remains. It's like an iceberg in the ocean—barely hidden below the surface, and deadly.

Here Paul focuses on the ways we reveal anger. Not unlike Ephesians 4:31 (recall day 6), this passage lists a half-dozen or so anger-like terms: enmity, strife, jealousy, fits of anger, rivalries, dissensions, and divisions.

What do all these words have in common? They are relational. They have to do with how we relate to and interact with others. In fact, today's text immediately follows the apostle's warning that "if you bite and devour each other, watch out or you will be destroyed by each other" (Gal. 5:15). Anger ruins relationships. What might revealed anger look like? We have heard it with our ears and expressed it with our mouths: cynical comments, calculated criticism, loud voices, sharp tongues, expletives. We have seen it with our eyes and done it with our actions: throwing blows, slamming doors, storming away from an argument, grabbing someone forcefully. I have certainly said and done things I regret. What about you?

There is no limit to the ways we might let others feel our wrath. We desperately need the Holy Spirit to fight for us and to help us.

Reflect: What does your revealed anger look like? Do you feel guilt or shame for your anger? If so, run to Christ for mercy and forgiveness.

Reflect: The Bible records hundreds of stories of revealed anger. Consider Potiphar in Genesis 39, Moses in Numbers 20, David in 2 Samuel 12, Herod in Matthew 2, and the scribes and Pharisees in various Gospel narratives.

Act: Memorize Galatians 5:16—"Walk by the Spirit, and you will not gratify the desires of the flesh"—and run to it the moment you are tempted to express anger toward someone. Ask God's Spirit to guard your heart and to control your words and actions.

DAY 20

What Revealed Anger Looks Like

*The wise fear the LORD and shun evil, but a fool is hotheaded and
yet feels secure. A quick-tempered person does foolish things, and
the one who devises evil schemes is hated. (Prov. 14:16–17)*

*Whoever is patient has great understanding, but one who is
quick-tempered displays folly. A heart at peace gives life to
the body, but envy rots the bones. (Prov. 14:29–30)*

A MIRROR SHOWS us what we look like—for good or for
ill. We might not like what we see, but it often motivates us to
improve ourselves. (This very morning, as I write this, I see my
desperate need for a haircut.)

What does an angry person look like? Our verses from Proverbs 14 supply some disturbing images.

*1. When we display our anger, God calls us hotheaded, quick-
tempered people.* We might naively feel confident and secure, but
our impatient, impulsive, reckless behavior betrays the opposite
and puts us in spiritual and sometimes physical danger.

2. Angry people are fools. Don't envision a "fool" in Proverbs as a
jovial buffoon. He is ungodly. His behavior does not invite laughs;
it invites pity. He is hated by others and under God's judgment.

These verses sober us when we willingly recognize such
descriptions as applying to us. Amid our occasional or chronic
rage episodes, the Lord calls us to label ourselves as hotheaded,
quick-tempered fools. When we do so, we are more likely to take
our sin seriously and become wise men and women who fear God
and shun evil.[1] We must see our sin as God sees it.

3. A fool acts foolishly. Fools do evil things, such as mocking
and hating God's truth (see Prov. 1:22, 29); spreading slander
(see 10:18); enjoying wicked schemes (see 10:23); blurting folly

and delighting in airing their own opinions (see 12:23; 15:2; 18:2); bringing grief, ruin, and heartache to their mothers and fathers (see 10:1; 15:20; 17:21, 25; 19:13); creating strife in relationships (see 18:6); failing to do anything useful (see 26:6–12); giving full vent to their anger (see 29:9, 11); and committing many sins (see 29:22).

4. *Anger impacts the body.* The Bible makes a connection between anger/impatience and bone-rotting psychosomatic problems. Medical research shows a correlation between anger and high blood pressure, headaches, and gastrointestinal symptoms. (Ask your primary care physician how often he or she sees this.) Learning to overcome anger and live at peace can bring renewed health to both your soul and your body.

While I can think of people who fit these four descriptions, I can also think of people who have owned, repented of, and are in the process of changing these vices. I was one of them.

How about you? Do you see your anger as God sees it? Are you a hotheaded, quick-tempered fool? Are you impatient, impulsive, or reckless? Do you scream, slam doors, or throw things? Do you make sarcastic, biting, or cutting comments? Or do you instead seek the Lord's help in manifesting Spirit-empowered self-control?

Praise God when fools become wise through faith in Jesus.

Reflect: Proverbs contains rich imagery related to anger—and especially revealed anger. Consider these vivid passages: 12:18; 15:1, 18; 16:32; 19:11, 19; 22:24–25. Let one or two of them capture your imagination and guide you to deepening repentance and faith.

Act: When you are tempted to display anger, look in the mirror of Proverbs 14, pray, and seek accountability *before* your anger heats up and rules your heart. Don't fight this battle alone!

DAY 21

Concealed Anger and Grudge-Bearing

Do not hate a fellow Israelite in your heart. Rebuke your neighbor frankly so you will not share in their guilt. Do not seek revenge or bear a grudge against anyone among your people, but love your neighbor as yourself. I am the LORD. (Lev. 19:17–18)

SOME OF US have learned to cover our anger well. We keep it under wraps and avoid outward displays so that others won't see or suspect it. However, like revealed anger, concealed anger offends God, ruins relationships, and must be replaced.

What does God say about anger that outwardly seems controlled but inwardly simmers? Nestled within Levitical law are several relational commands that look like New Testament "one another" verses. Let's consider two that relate to concealed anger.

1. You must not hate your brother or sister in your heart. Leviticus 19 syncs with what we have repeatedly seen: hatred starts in the heart (see Matt. 5:21–22 from day 4 and 1 John 3:15 from day 5). Instead of bringing a wise, needed rebuke to offenders, we make secret judgments and harbor unvoiced rebukes inside. We internally confront them, declare them guilty, and imprison them—while outwardly displaying social decorum.

2. You must not bear a grudge. This command translates a single Hebrew verb that often means "keep" or "harbor." When we bear grudges, we keep offenders and their offenses ever before our eyes, allowing resentment to breed. It's the precise opposite of the way that the Lord treats us: "He will not always accuse, nor will he harbor his anger forever" (Ps. 103:9). God doesn't bear grudges against his people. Because of Jesus's death on the cross, God doesn't keep his anger or hold our offenses before his eyes.

The remedy to hating others in our hearts and bearing grudges? Love your neighbor as you love yourself—the same command that Jesus and his apostles frequently repeat. This, of course, is not a command to love yourself—we already do this too deeply and too often. Instead, we must love and serve others in the same way that we instinctively seek our own welfare.

Why? Verse 18 clinches it with a simple, sobering reminder: "I am the LORD." The presence of the Lord—our covenant-keeping King and Redeemer—constrains us toward loving obedience.

What do we need most in times when we are concealing our anger? To draw near to the Lord and imitate him. We must know him as the one who loves us, not hates us, in his heart, and who commands and enables us to do the same in our hearts toward others. He bears no grudges against us but in Christ brings us his unending, inexhaustible riches.

Reflect: Perhaps the saddest biblical display of concealed anger appears in Luke 15. After the good news of the prodigal son's return and the festive joy of the father, the pharisaical older brother "became angry and refused" to enter the house and join the celebration (v. 28). Compare this story with our Leviticus passage and with passages like 1 Corinthians 13:5 and Ephesians 4:26–27.[1]

Reflect: Because of Jesus, God doesn't bear a grudge against you. Are you ready to do the same—to draw near to the Lord and imitate him?

Act: When you are tempted to go underground with your anger, the first person you must talk to is not yourself or your offender but your Lord. Go to him immediately. Ask him to give you a gracious heart toward that person and wisdom for how to pursue relational peace.

DAY 22

Don't Get Mad; Get a Grip!

Better a patient person than a warrior, one with self-control than one who takes a city. (Prov. 16:32)

Like a city whose walls are broken through is a person who lacks self-control. (Prov. 25:28)

Fools give full vent to their rage, but the wise bring calm in the end. (Prov. 29:11)

WE'VE ALL HEARD the motto "Don't get mad; get even!" While we reject that ungodly counsel, it reminds us not to remain in a perpetual state of anger but to do something. For the next few devotionals we will focus on what to do. What are the godly replacements for sinful anger—the "put on" components in our put-off/put-on dynamic (see Eph. 4:22–24)?

As all Proverbs do, our three Spirit-given verses are concise one-liners that pack a piercing punch. Proverbs 16:32 tells us where real strength lies—not in capturing a city but in capturing your own soul. True strength in God's eyes means victory over one's temper more than over one's enemies. The humble believer who exercises self-control is mightier than the greatest Olympic weightlifter. Before God, that "tough guy" who explodes with pounding fists is a moral wimp. What kind of strength do you exude? What kind do you prize and pursue?

Proverbs 25:28 is equally striking. People in ancient Near Eastern cities depended on stone walls to shield them from raiding bandits, vicious wolves, and conquering armies. In the same way, this verse vividly reminds us that uncontrolled anger invites invasion from our spiritual enemies. It makes us easy prey for the world, the flesh, and the devil.

I counseled a man who came home from work one day to find that his teenage son had failed to do several chores he had promised to do. On discovering this, the man raced up the stairs, burst into his son's room, and went off on a tirade. As the man described his rage, all I could picture were all the walls of his life breaking down as he ran up the steps and the enemies of God assaulting his unprotected soul as he verbally assaulted his son. What kind of walls of self-control have you erected? What are you doing to repair and strengthen them? Your walls against temptation will not build themselves; you must be vigilant and nurture godly self-control in your life.

Proverbs 29:11 provides a third image. When we lose control and vent our anger, we act like fools. This description should sober us. Owning the label of being a fool is our first step toward true repentance. In contrast, the wise person remains calm. Wisdom in the Old Testament denotes skill in godly practical living, and wise people know how to control their tongues and exercise self-restraint. When it comes to your anger, are you more foolish or wise?

Reflect: Read Galatians 5:22–23. The ninefold fruit of the Spirit includes self-control—the relational grace we have meditated on above. In the coming days, we will consider more replacements for anger that will map on to this Galatians 5 list. Remember that all this fruit is the work of the Holy Spirit. Praise him for what he produces.

Act: Fasten your mind on one or more of the images in the Proverbs above. When you become angry, recite that verse three times, and seize the image. Rebuke yourself as a "fool" and repent. Envision yourself as a wise man or woman, practice the positive command, and ask God's Spirit to give you his fruit of self-control.

DAY 23

Don't Get Mad; Get Patient!

*A hot-tempered person stirs up conflict, but the one
who is patient calms a quarrel. (Prov. 15:18)*

*A person's wisdom yields patience; it is to one's glory
to overlook an offense. (Prov. 19:11)*

"PATIENCE IS A virtue—possess it if you can—seldom found
in woman, never found in man." Whatever truth might lie in that
admittedly sexist saying, the Bible provides equal-gender judgment and equal-gender hope. It attributes the sin of impatience to
all people but promises in Galatians 5:22 that any Christian man
or woman who walks by the Spirit can demonstrate patience—
the fruit of God's Spirit.

Our pair of Proverbs verses for today underscores the value of
putting off anger and putting on patience.

Proverbs 15:18 makes a wise observation: when you lose
your temper, you provoke anger from others. Their anger, in turn,
invites an angry counter-response from you, and the cycle starts.
Calmness evaporates; conflict escalates. It no longer matters who
started it, as each of you tries to end it by winning the fight.

The same verse, however, holds out for us a different vision:
giving patient responses—being "slow to anger" (ESV)—can
calm a quarrel. Patience short-circuits the charged situation and
deescalates the tension. While walking away, counting to ten (or
two hundred), or putting your head in the freezer for ten seconds
might help, recalling this passage first and asking the Holy Spirit
for immediate help are even better.

Our second verse takes us further. Christlike wisdom makes
us patient, and patient people are forgiving people. Instead of

becoming irritated, wise and patient people overlook the sins of others.[1] What does it mean to overlook sin? The Hebrew verb indicates movement and typically means to pass by or pass over. In this context, it carries the sense of forgiving (see also 2 Sam. 12:13; Mic. 7:18). When I walk in the Spirit's wisdom, I patiently put up with your failures. I look over, past, and beyond them, as Christ has done for mine (see Ps. 103:12). I choose not to remember them.[2]

Moreover, Proverbs 19:11 tells us that overlooking sins is a glorious act of grace. While it's an evil act to cover your own sins (see Prov. 28:13), it's a glorious act when God overlooks someone else's sins and when you, his son or daughter, follow his example!

Reflect: What counsel does our culture give for handling anger? When I searched for "Anger Management" on the web, the two top articles that came up were "Anger Management: 10 Tips to Tame Your Temper," from the Mayo Clinic,[3] and "Controlling Anger before It Controls You," from the American Psychological Association.[4] Yet no secular counsel compares to the grace of Jesus Christ, the truth of God's Word, the power of God's Spirit, and the ministry of a vibrant local church. (On a more humorous note, my all-time favorite bits of calming counsel from television shows and films are "Enhance your calm!";[5] "Serenity now!";[6] and "I Feel Pretty."[7])

Act: Relational *patience* promotes relational *peace*. Consider the potentially tense situations you face—to whom do you need to show extra measures of patience in these situations? Ask the Lord to grant you patience through his Spirit, and ask for prayer, counsel, and accountability from a pastor or a mature Christian friend.

DAY 24

Don't Get Mad; Get Talking!

The words of the reckless pierce like swords, but the tongue of the wise brings healing. (Prov. 12:18)

A gentle answer turns away wrath, but a harsh word stirs up anger. (Prov. 15:1)

If a wise person goes to court with a fool, the fool rages and scoffs, and there is no peace. (Prov. 29:9)

OUR TRIO OF Proverbs for today have one commonality: they all connect anger with ungodly speech. Sinful anger produces sinful words, and sinful words provoke further sinful anger.

Proverbs 12:18 contrasts two kinds of speech and the impacts that result from both of them. While the word *reckless* (or *rash*, in the ESV) generally indicates thoughtless speech, here it implies angry speech (see Ps. 106:33, where it is used of Moses's angry words) because of the direct harm that such speech does to its recipient. Reckless words pierce people like sword thrusts.

Have you ever aimed angry words at someone else? Perhaps you justified it in your mind: "I just have to get something off my chest." Whose chest do you most care about? To speak rashly in order to get things off your chest is to impale the chest of the other person. Sharp tongues cut deeply.

The antidote to reckless words are wise words that bring healing: words that encourage, comfort, and counsel others with godly wisdom.

Proverbs 15:1 recognizes a dynamic that we all have experienced. We are having a conversation that involves a difference of opinion. Both participants value their viewpoint, and we each dig in our heels. One person then voices a harsh word. Our voices rise. It escalates to a heated argument and then to a yelling match. We might go to our separate corners, but the fight remains unresolved. Another sun goes down on another unresolved conflict (see Eph. 4:26–27).

What can interrupt the cycle and lower the temperature? A soft, gentle answer. A calmly spoken word from a gracious, self-controlled heart can quickly de-escalate a fight. When one person chooses a soft answer, the other person, instead of continuing the path of anger, now follows the path of peace. Harsh words stir up anger; soft words decrease it.

Our last verse, Proverbs 29:9, continues our theme. Arguing with a fool is unproductive. When you try to engage with a fool on a serious relational issue, he or she either rages or laughs, and conflict ensues.

How do you respond when someone confronts you? Do you lash out and rage, or do you softly and humbly receive the rebuke?

In light of these three verses, how wise and productive is your speech—especially when a conversation gets tense? Do you bring wise, healing words or rash sword-thrusts? Do you speak softly or harshly? Do you discuss your differences with others in productive ways or in angry or sarcastic ways?

In your fight against anger, as another Proverb puts it, "The tongue has the power of life and death" (18:21).

Reflect: Along with Proverbs 12:18 and 15:1 above, my favorite go-to passage about godly speech is Ephesians 4:29. Meditate on it in light of our trio of verses above and see how harmoniously they function together.

Act: When a conversation starts to get tense or heated, take the following steps: (1) Shut up. (2) Pray; ask God to help you respond wisely. (3) Speak calmly, graciously, and briefly. (4) Focus on relational love more than on winning the argument.

DAY 25

Don't Get Mad; Get Gracious!

But now you must also rid yourselves of all such things as these: anger, rage, malice, slander, and filthy language from your lips.... Therefore, as God's chosen people, holy and dearly loved, clothe yourselves with compassion, kindness, humility, gentleness and patience. Bear with each other and forgive one another if any of you has a grievance against someone. Forgive as the Lord forgave you. And over all these virtues put on love, which binds them all together in perfect unity. (Col. 3:8, 12–14)

ON DAY 6, we saw Paul's call to us, in Ephesians 4:31, to get rid of all forms of anger and to replace them with forgiving grace. Let's consider today's parallel passage from Colossians 3.

Paul begins the chapter by reminding believers of our union with the risen, reigning Christ and by calling us to set our minds and hearts on the realities that lie above with him (see vv. 1–4). In light of our resurrected status and the new life we have received (see vv. 10–11)—no self-help here—the apostle calls us in verses 5–9 to put to death our remaining sins, because they belong to our old selves and invite God's impending judgment.

Our old selves' sinful patterns include the various forms of anger that he mentions in verse 8, which are similar to the six terms he mentions in Ephesians 4:31. While the lists largely overlap, they are not identical or exhaustive (especially when we ponder the Proverbs passages we have recently seen).

In Colossians 3:12–14, Paul highlights four saving realities of our new identity: We have been *chosen*—chosen, by sheer grace, by our triune God who set his saving love on us before the foundation of the earth. We are *holy*—set apart by God as his special possession (which is the meaning of *holy* here) to belong to Christ and become like Christ. We are *deeply loved*—God demonstrated

71

his affection supremely when he "rescued us from the dominion of darkness and brought us into the kingdom of the Son he loves" (Col. 1:13). We are *forgiven*—God's work canceled our debt to him: "When you were dead in your sins and in the uncircumcision of your flesh, God made you alive with Christ. He forgave us all our sins" (Col. 2:13).

Since this is who we now are in Christ, we can and must live out this new identity, following the eight relational graces in verses 12–14—the godly replacements for the sins we must put off. Notice the flow:

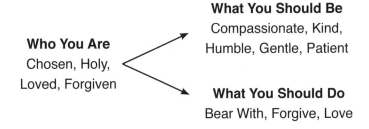

What You Should Be
Compassionate, Kind, Humble, Gentle, Patient

Who You Are
Chosen, Holy, Loved, Forgiven

What You Should Do
Bear With, Forgive, Love

You are defined by who you are in Christ, not by your anger. Fight to remember this truth.

Reflect: If God has dealt with sinners like us so graciously, how can we not be gracious toward those who offend us today?

Reflect: Contrast the relational sins in verse 8 with the relational graces in verses 12–14. What traits will you put on in place of anger?

Act: When tempted toward anger, remind yourself of who you are and to whom you belong. Let that dictate what you should do and how you should act. Plead with God to help you respond graciously.

DAY 26

Don't Get Mad; Get Reconciled!

*"Therefore, if you are offering your gift at the altar and there remember
that your brother or sister has something against you, leave your gift
there in front of the altar. First go and be reconciled." (Matt. 5:23–24)*

*"If your brother or sister sins, go and point out their fault, just between the
two of you. If they listen to you, you have won them over." (Matt. 18:15)*

LET'S ADMIT IT—ANGER ruins relationships. Perhaps in
your anger you sinned against a Christian brother or sister, and
that person has pulled away from you. Or perhaps someone has
sinned against you, and you are simmering inside. Thankfully, our
Lord addresses both of these scenarios.

In Matthew 5:23–24, after having addressed the heart problem of anger in the preceding verses (see day 4), Jesus gives concrete counsel on what you should do if someone has been offended
by you. If someone has something against you, you should go to
that person to seek reconciliation. In an arresting way, Jesus pri-
oritizes relational peace above other acts of worship—"leave your
gift" and "first" go to the person. As someone has asked, what
would happen if we invented an unresolved-conflict detector and
installed one at the entrance of every church building so we could
keep out those who haven't pursued peace in their relationships?
I wonder what Sunday morning attendance might look like.

Sadly, we concoct various ways to escape our Lord's call.
We might modify Jesus's words to say, "Go only if someone has
something *big* against you"—as if only major issues matter. Issues
that seem minor to you might not be minor to another person.
Or we want Jesus to say, "Go only if your brother has something
justifiable against you"—as if you can infallibly decide what's right
and wrong.

It's much easier to leave a relationship behind than to own our sin and repent, but that's not the life Jesus calls us to pursue in the church. If your sister or brother has anything against you, you must deal with it—even if you think it's small or unfair. Matthew 18:15 reverses the scene. What if a brother or sister has sinned against you?[1] Based on what we saw on day 23—that Scripture calls us to overlook minor offenses—we can assume that the sin here is something serious and something that the person has not dealt with. The counsel for addressing the sin carries the same goal as the counsel in Matthew 5: reconciliation.

What do these passages have to do with your anger? It's simple: if you are angry with someone or if your anger has offended someone, then you must take the first step to reconcile the relationship. While you could hope that the other person would heed Christ's counsel themselves, you must not wait for that. Whether they do or don't, you should go yourself.

Reflect: Our Lord's twofold command for you to seek reconciliation—whether you are the offender or the offended—powerfully illustrates Romans 12:18: "If it is possible, as far as it depends on you, live at peace with everyone." While this text does not guarantee reconciliation, it requires you to make every effort to seek it. Think of relational tensions that you currently face. What would a Romans 12:18 commitment look like?

Reflect: What things get in your way of initiating reconciliation? What fears are stopping you? What rationalizations are you using in order to escape a hard conversation?

Act: Follow Jesus's commands. Whatever your conflict scenario, go to the other person. If you need counsel, seek it from your church leaders or wise friends who understand biblical peacemaking.

Don't Get Mad; Get Content!

I have learned to be content whatever the circumstances. I know
what it is to be in need, and I know what it is to have plenty. I have
learned the secret of being content in any and every situation, whether
well fed or hungry, whether living in plenty or in want. I can do
all this through him who gives me strength. (Phil. 4:11–13)

AS WE HAVE seen previously, anger arises in our hearts in
response to situations that we don't like. Today, let's focus on still
another replacement we can put on: learning to be content in
those unfavorable situations that tempt us to become angry.

Paul wrote to the Philippians, in part, to thank them for the
financial gift they had recently sent him. In verse 10, he tells how
he rejoiced in the Lord for their evident care for him. Yet in our
passage above, he wants to clarify his mindset. Whatever his
circumstances might be—whether he is in financial need or in
plenty, whether he is well supported or unsupported—Paul has
learned to be content.

What is contentment? It is believing that God is good when
our situation is not. It is finding inner satisfaction in God alone
and in his provisions for us. It is that God-given sense of well-be-
ing, peace, and confidence that we can have in any circumstance.
As Puritan minister Jeremiah Burroughs put it, it is "that sweet,
inward, quiet, gracious frame of spirit, which freely submits to and
delights in God's wise and fatherly disposal in every situation."[1]

We learn from these verses a hope-expanding truth: your
contentment does not depend on your circumstances. It comes
from God. In verse 13, Paul refers to God: "I can do all this
[i.e., live contentedly] through him." But he doesn't stop there:
"through him *who gives me strength*." The apostle singles out this

one specific attribute of God. He depends on God's power to enable him to handle hard times—on God's enabling grace, his "grace to help us in our time of need" (see Heb. 4:16 from day 3). Contentment, however, does not happen automatically. It must be learned. Paul stresses this by using two different but synonymous Greek terms for learning. Growing in contentment is a process—a part of your progressive maturation as a Christian.

Most of our angry reactions come when someone doesn't treat us the way we want to be treated or when some circumstance goes against our desires. It's at this point—at this fork in the road—that we can choose either anger or contentment.

Reflect: People sometimes think of a smiling, cooing baby as a picture of contentment, but take away his favorite toy or put her down when she wants to be held, and all that baby's contentment quickly vanishes. Picture instead an old, weatherbeaten, hungry apostle sitting in a dungeon singing praise to his Savior. Take away Paul's favorite toy and he still finds joy in Jesus Christ! Set him down when he doesn't want you to and he prays for you! The apostle has learned contentment despite severe hardships. Which image of contentment—a happy baby or an imprisoned apostle—best describes you? Which do you long for?

Act: At the specific point when your relationships or circumstances tempt you to become angry, ask God to help you learn what Paul learned—that God's strength can enable you to learn contentment "in any and every situation."

ANGER AT YOURSELF, GOD, AND CHILDREN

DAY 28

Anger at Yourself

I consider everything a loss because of the surpassing worth of knowing Christ Jesus my Lord, for whose sake I have lost all things. I consider them garbage, that I may gain Christ and be found in him, not having a righteousness of my own that comes from the law, but that which is through faith in Christ—the righteousness that comes from God on the basis of faith. (Phil. 3:8–9)

"I CAN'T BELIEVE I said that." "I could kick myself for how I acted." "What on earth was I thinking when I made that decision?" Have you ever said or thought things like this? These are verdicts—moral judgments—that you make about your actions or inactions. You are angry at you.[1]

What's going on when this happens? Perhaps you are unable or unwilling to acknowledge and own the depth of your sin or to grasp and receive the heights of God's forgiveness. Maybe you have ascended the throne of judgment, displaced God, and declared yourself to be your own (unforgiving) judge.[2] Perhaps you are venting your regrets for failing to achieve some cherished desire. Had you acted differently, you would have received some benefit. But now it's gone because of your failure. Your wrong choice then has cost you deeply now. The desires that drove you then (see James 4:1), and the decisions that flowed from them, now interfere with your current desires.

But there's another possible cause of self-anger—one that our passage speaks to. Perhaps you are seeking to establish and live under your own standards of righteousness. Maybe you have invented laws out of your perfectionism ("Good moms read five books a day to their children") or have adopted as your own the standards that others have sought to impose on you ("Son, you should do that chore perfectly"). You have proudly erected your own law or fearfully embraced someone else's law. Either way, your standards are higher than or different from God's. And when you fail to achieve them, you judge yourself and become angry at yourself.

Paul understood the danger of living under a law (in his case, the old covenant—the law of Moses) that was no longer God's law in the new covenant. Instead of living under that law, he explains in today's passage that he now pursues a different righteousness—one that comes from God and depends on faith. Self-anger comes when you pursue a "righteousness of [your] own" that is built on standards of your own. When you succeed, you swell with pride and self-righteousness, as Paul did earlier in this chapter. When you fail, you attack yourself in anger or sink into depression.

The ultimate problem is not your behavior but the unbiblical law that you have adopted and sought to follow. The answer is the gospel of Jesus Christ.

Reflect: What unbiblical standards have you adopted? How have they led you to be unduly critical of yourself? What, instead, does God's Word say about this matter?

Reflect: The church of Jesus has long recognized Philippians 3:1–14 as a crucial passage for understanding not only Paul's conversion but also a central Bible doctrine: justification by faith. Take some time to review this passage in order to remind yourself that saving righteousness comes from God (and not from the law), that it is found only in Christ, and that we receive it solely by faith and not by works.

Act: When you find that you are angry at yourself, ask yourself why. Your anger likely stems from one of the causes above. Once you have determined the error that your anger is founded on, bring the gospel's truths to bear on that error.

DAY 29

Don't Blame God—It's Blasphemy

*[Job] said: "Naked I came from my mother's womb, and naked
I will depart. The LORD gave and the LORD has taken away;
may the name of the LORD be praised." In all this, Job did not
sin by charging God with wrongdoing. (Job 1:21–22)*

*His wife said to him, "Are you still maintaining your integrity? Curse
God and die!" He replied, ". . . Shall we accept good from God, and not
trouble?" In all this, Job did not sin in what he said. (Job 2:9–10)*

IS IT RIGHT, or is it wrong, to be angry with God? It's a question that some people avoid. They don't believe in God, they don't see him as being involved in suffering, or they don't see him as the ultimate King who is sovereign over every incident, person, and molecule in the universe. But for those who hold a high view of God's sovereignty,[1] the question remains relevant. Why does God allow us to suffer? Why didn't he stop my child's death, my spouse's infidelity, my job loss, or my cancer? Such anger is understandable. But is it right?

In Job 1–2, Job and his wife both suffer severely. They suddenly lose all their great wealth and all ten of their children. Job is then inflicted with an awful skin disease that produces painful boils from head to toe.

They not only both suffer severely but also both know that God ultimately permitted their suffering.[2]

However, they each respond to this knowledge differently. Job trusts God; Mrs. Job rejects God. And from their different hearts come different words.[3] He praises God; his wife curses God.

Their story reminds us that severe suffering cannot cause you to sin or prevent you from obeying.

If, as we have defined it previously, anger is a whole-person response of negative moral judgment against perceived evil, then our question has been answered: it is wrong to be angry at God, because that requires you to judge God as an evildoer. That's blasphemy. We must reject any insinuation that denies God's goodness, power, and wisdom, and we must reaffirm his righteousness, love, and justice—even amid suffering.

Consider John Calvin's keen pastoral insight: "Job attributed to God nothing without reason, that is to say, he did not imagine that God did anything which was not just and equitable. . . . As soon as God does not send what we have desired, we dispute against him, we bring suit. . . . It is as if [people] accused God of being a tyrant or a hair-brain. . . . Such horrible blasphemy blows out of the mouths of men."[4]

Our Job 1–2 passage warns us to not blame God in the midst of our troubles. When you suffer, to what degree do you find yourself responding like Job . . . or like Mrs. Job?

Reflect: In times of severe hardship, in what ways do you sometimes blame God—even subtly?

Reflect: Read Job 1:1–2:7 in order to better understand the story above. Other people in the Bible got angry with God and expressed it, such as Cain (see Gen. 4), David (see 1 Chron. 13), Jonah (who even justified it—see Jonah 4), or the Jewish crowd (see John 7:23). Compare and contrast each of these people with Job and his wife, and consider Calvin's comments.

Act: When you find anger against God rising inside you, ask yourself what this anger says about God—about his character, ways, attributes, and heart. Repent of your accusation. (And read about the biblical alternative of lamenting that tomorrow offers!) Your pastor or a Christian leader can likely help you to gain a clearer view of God.

DAY 30

Don't Blame God; Learn to Lament

How long, LORD, must I call for help, but you do not listen? Or cry out to you, "Violence!" but you do not save? Why do you make me look at injustice? Why do you tolerate wrongdoing? (Hab. 1:2–3)

Though the fig tree does not bud and there are no grapes on the vines, though the olive crop fails and the fields produce no food, though there are no sheep in the pen and no cattle in the stalls, yet I will rejoice in the LORD, I will be joyful in God my Savior. The Sovereign LORD is my strength. (Hab. 3:17–19)

WE SAW YESTERDAY that to be angry at God is to accuse him of evil. So what should you do if you face hardships that you didn't cause and that yield no obvious explanation—when God allows suffering that seems unjust, unfair, and unloving?

The answer: lament! Lamenting involves expressing to God in prayer your confusion, your pain, and your fear over what he is (or isn't) doing amid your suffering. Today's passage provides a moving example. On the eve of Babylon's invasion of Israel, Habakkuk voices his honest complaints to God about why God is sovereignly using an ungodly nation to discipline his people (see Hab. 1:1–4, 12–2:1).

What elements of biblical laments do we see?[1]

1. Suffering. Lamenters in the Bible not only suffer but also wrestle over apparent inconsistencies between God's revealed character and his current providential dealings.

2. Prayer. Believers voice their questions directly to God. They move *toward* God, not *away from* him. They talk *to* God, not *about* him.

3. Faith. The laments of believers arise from a fundamental (albeit imperfect) faith. In the trenches, they submit to God and cling to his Word. In fact, it's their belief in God's absolute sovereignty, power, wisdom, and goodness that occasions their complaints in the first place! The mindset sounds like this: "Father, it's precisely *because* I know that you are all-loving and all-powerful that I am struggling with the seeming absence of your love and power right now. It's *because* I am convinced that you are good that your chastening and apparent distance baffle me. I really need your help."

4. *Humility.* Believers express their laments with reverence and submission. They don't vent or lose control. By humbling themselves, they avoid the blasphemous accusations that are found in pagan religious literature. They are crying out for help, not shaking their fists.

5. *Renewal.* Believers reach some resolution of their struggle: a faith that is tried and tested and made riper and sweeter through the hardship. Habakkuk's conclusion in 3:17–19 expresses a profound, joyous, growing faith in the Lord himself, despite the prophet's desolate circumstances (as in Gen. 50:20; Rom. 8:28).

You are not alone in the trials that tempt you toward anger. God invites you to talk to him, whatever your circumstances or mood. Therefore, learn to lament. When your circumstances are hard, or when something provokes you to anger, go immediately to God in prayer.

Reflect: In hardship, do you turn *to* God or *away from* God?

Reflect: Read Habakkuk in one sitting and note the five components of lament in it. For further study, read and reflect on the book of Lamentations or on a lament Psalm such as Psalm 13. The closing sections of Job, Lamentations, Habakkuk, and Psalm 13 all reflect maturing faith.

Act: Write out a lament to God—one that models honesty, faith, and humility.

DAY 31

A Plea to Parents
(and All Who Love Children)

*Do not make friends with a hot-tempered person, do not
associate with one easily angered, or you may learn their
ways and get yourself ensnared. (Prov. 22:24–25)*

I SAT IN the living room of a young married couple who had
small children. They had a copy of my *Uprooting Anger* book on
their shelf. The mom explained to her two-year-old daughter that
I had written the book. The mom then asked her daughter if she
knew anyone who gets angry. The girl quickly replied, "Mommy."
We all laughed.

In my thirty-five years of pastoring and counseling parents,
I've never met any who don't sometimes exhibit sinful anger—
especially with their tongues. James reminds us that "we all stumble in many ways" before applying this assertion to our sinful
speech (James 3:2).

Today's passage from Proverbs urges us to avoid hanging out
with hot-tempered people. Why? Because angry friends model
anger and tempt you toward it yourself.[1] Angry people can influence you in subtle and ensnaring ways. Anger can be contagious.

But what if that angry person is your mom or dad—someone
whom you can't avoid and whose angry influence is inescapable?
What if you had to endure eighteen years of verbal attack?

If you are a parent or have any involvement with children, I
plead with you to deal with your anger.

A friend shared with me his fear that, in his anger, he might
someday hurt one of his children. His fears made sense—he has
a vivid childhood memory of being thrown down by his mother.
My friend isn't alone—though I'm not talking primarily about

physical violence, as evil as that is. I'm talking about demeaning speech, name-calling, sarcasm, and critical comments—those reckless words that pierce like a sword (see Prov. 12:18 from day 24). You might not intend to have a negative influence on your child. Most parents don't. But inadvertent, unintentional anger is still sinful and harmful.

Of course, the gospel brings good news: even if you grew up with angry parents, you are not doomed. And if you are an angry parent, your children are not doomed. Christ has come to redeem us from the sinful patterns that were handed down to us from our ancestors (see 1 Peter 1:18). While parental anger is influential, because of Christ and his Spirit within you it is not determinative. There is hope for you, and for your kids, if you repent of your anger and seek to change.

Reflect: Consider Ephesians 6:4: "Fathers, do not provoke your children to anger, but bring them up in the discipline and instruction of the Lord" (ESV). While this verse singles out fathers (as the head of the home), the rest of the Bible calls both mothers and fathers to engage in godly parenting. This verse warns us against actions we might wrongly take that can provoke (i.e., tempt or invite—not cause or determine) children to become angry.

Reflect: If you have been angry with your kids, do you need to seek their forgiveness?

Act: If you are a parent, grandparent, childcare provider, or someone who works with children, immediately seek God's help when you—inevitably—feel anger toward them. If you need to distance yourself at the moment, do so. Ask your spouse, if you are married, or other adults to privately tell you if you are showing anger toward your children. Ask them to hold you accountable. Or ask your children, if you dare.

Conclusion: Where Should You Go Now and Why?

CONGRATULATIONS! YOU HAVE completed our thirty-one-day devotional journey. During this trip, you met daily with God in prayer and experienced the timely help of his Holy Spirit. You learned each day, from Scripture, how to think accurately about your anger, how to respond to the temptations that persistently provoke your anger, and how to put off your anger and put on godly replacements. Along the way you have also pondered topics like righteous anger (God's and your own), anger against God, and anger against yourself.

Next Steps

While you have completed this one journey, you now start a bigger journey—one that will continue for the rest of your life. That journey involves cultivating a growing relationship with the Lord and applying his Word in fresh and flourishing ways.

How should you progress? Where should you go from here? Let me suggest six big-picture steps.

1. Reread this book, or at least the days that you found particularly useful. The short, two-page length of these entries allows you to review them quickly as needed.
2. If you have not done so along the way, write down key Scripture memory passages on 3x5 cards (or using the electronic method you prefer) and post them in your home, car, or workplace, or carry them around with you for frequent review.
3. Read the recommended book and booklet resources at the end of this book. All of these are relatively short and are written at a popular level by biblical counseling practitioners.

4. If you haven't done so, find and join a solid gospel-driven church. Immerse yourself into its full life. There you will experience Christ-centered corporate worship—including singing, prayer, the Lord's Supper, and the reading and exposition of God's Word. A healthy church family will assimilate you into small-group life, where you can develop meaningful friendships with other people who need and are together learning God's grace. This fellowship will allow you to pursue accountability as you confide in trusted church leaders about your struggles with anger.

5. If your anger is steadily getting worse instead of better, consider counseling. A gospel-centered church can provide, or point you to, biblical counseling help as it is needed. Be humble enough to ask for assistance.

6. Renew your spiritual disciplines of prayer and Bible reading. Commit yourself to regularly praying for God to help you fight your anger. While our thirty-one days have given you a disciplined way to read and apply God's Word and to commune with the Lord, you need to develop your own lifelong rhythms and habits.

Remember that our goal at the outset of our trip was steady progress, not immediate elimination. These steps will encourage that ongoing growth.

Four Reasons to Fight against Your Anger[1]

Why should you continue this new path?

Your Anger Hurts Your Health

You should deal biblically with your anger because your anger hurts your personal physical and spiritual health. We noted the potential connection that Proverbs 14:30 draws between anger and physical disease on day 20 (see also Ps. 32; 38; Prov. 3). But there are spiritual consequences, as well, that sin—including anger—brings.

- a disrupted conscience (see Acts 24:16)
- hindered prayers (see Ps. 66:18; 1 Tim. 2:8; 1 Peter 3:7)
- God's judgment (see Matt. 5:21–22)
- slavery to ongoing sin (see Gen. 4:6–7)

Your Anger Ruins Your Relationships

You should also deal biblically with your anger because your anger ruins your relationships. Several of the Bible's clearest calls to get rid of anger (e.g., Eph. 4:26–27, 31; Col. 3:8) come in contexts that focus on interpersonal relationships within the body of Christ. The various forms of anger that are prohibited in these verses disturb the peace, unity, and one-another ministry of Jesus's church. We see the same dynamic in James 3:13–4:12, where the apostle contrasts selfish ambition and its fruits, which include angry demands (see 4:1–2) and judgmentalism (see 4:11–12), with the heavenly wisdom that promotes relational love and peace with others (see 3:17–18). In all its forms, anger damages friendships, severs marriages, and alienates families. It keeps us from reconciling relationships and pursuing peace.

While these first two reasons should be sufficient to move us to carry out the biblical counsel we have seen, they are not the highest God-given motive.

Your Anger Offends Your God

Most importantly, you should deal biblically with your anger because your anger dishonors, offends, and grieves your God. Let's consider two key passages as we finish our journey.

In Ephesians 4:30, the apostle Paul exhorts us not to "grieve the Holy Spirit of God, with whom you were sealed for the day of redemption." How do you grieve God's Spirit? Verse 30 doesn't tell us, but verse 31 lists the behaviors that will, if we don't get rid of them: "all bitterness, rage and anger, brawling and slander, along with every form of malice." Instead, verse 32 continues, "Be kind and compassionate to one another, forgiving each other, just as in Christ God forgave you." You grieve God's Spirit when you fail to put off your sinful anger and fail to show kindness, compassion, and forgiveness.

In James 1:19, the apostle James pleads, "My dear brothers and sisters, take note of this: Everyone should be quick to liste n, slow to speak and slow to become angry." Why must you control your anger? To avoid high blood pressure, colitis, or a bad conscience? To avoid disrupted relationships, lost jobs, and broken homes? No—not according to this passage. In verse 20, James tells us why: "because human anger does not produce the righteousness that God desires."

When our hearts are angry, we fail to be and do what God has created and redeemed us to be and do. We dishonor the Savior who died, rose, and will return for us. We frustrate the Spirit's sanctifying purposes within us.

Your Anger Can Be Defeated

Finally, you should deal biblically with your anger because it is possible, with God's strength, to defeat this sin. You are not condemned to a lifetime of anger. Any lie that whispers to you, "This will never change," is just not true. By God's strength, and through the conviction and power of the Spirit, you can fight your anger problems. They don't have to have the final word. You can indeed approach God's throne of grace with confidence, knowing that from him you will surely "receive mercy and find grace to help us in our time of need" (Heb. 4:16).

Sister or brother, may God grant you increasing measures of his soul-calming peace in your fight against sinful anger.

The LORD bless you
and keep you;
the LORD make his face shine on you
and be gracious to you;
the LORD turn his face toward you
and give you peace.

Num. 6:24–26

Acknowledgments

LIKE EVERY CHRISTIAN author, I am dependent on my Creator and Redeemer for anything profitable that comes from my pen or keyboard. At various points I have felt the Lord standing by my side and giving me strength (see 2 Tim. 4:17). I am grateful for his unceasing grace.

I'm grateful to Deepak Reju for inviting me to write this book and to my friends at P&R for their fidelity to God's Word and for another opportunity to publish with them. Deepak's careful reading and editorial suggestions made this book more heart-searching and smoothed some rough edges. Amanda Martin's style assistance and content interaction further polished my work.

I am thankful to R. Albert Mohler, my seminary president; Randy Stinson, my seminary provost; Adam Greenway, my Billy Graham School dean; and the Board of Trustees of The Southern Baptist Theological Seminary for a sabbatical leave that provided me the time to complete this project.

I am grateful for the many men and women who over many years gave me the privilege of counseling them about their various forms and degrees of anger. I am honored that they have entrusted delicate parts of their lives with me. I have learned from them.

Special thanks go to two friends and fellow Third Avenue Baptist Church members, Bekka French and Lauren Whitmore, for their invaluable editorial help in the final stages of this book. Their combination of writing skill and biblical counseling insight made each day's devotional better than what I had originated.

And I am always thankful for my wife, Lauren, who for over thirty-five years has assisted me in uncountable ways and has modeled a calmed and calming heart despite the temptations to anger that I too often provide for her.

Notes

Tips for Reading This Devotional

1. Jonathan Leeman, *Reverberation: How God's Word Brings Light, Freedom, and Action to His People* (Chicago: Moody, 2011), 19.

Introduction

1. See Robert D. Jones, *Uprooting Anger: Biblical Help for a Common Problem* (Phillipsburg, NJ: P&R Publishing, 2005).

Day 1: You're Not Alone

1. Warren W. Wiersbe, *Be Patient: Waiting on God in Difficult Times* (1991; repr., Wheaton, IL: Victor Books, 1996), 94.

Day 2: Start with a Person, Not a Problem

1. J. A. Motyer, *The Message of James,* The Bible Speaks Today (Downers Grove, IL: InterVarsity Press, 1985), 187.
2. John Calvin, *Commentaries on the Catholic Epistles* (Bellingham, WA: Logos Bible Software, 2010), 354–55
3. Annie S. Hawks, "I Need Thee Every Hour," 1872.

Day 8: God's Wrath, Christ's Sacrifice, and Our Righteousness

1. For a clear, helpful explanation and application of Romans 3:19–26, see Jerry Bridges, "Preach the Gospel to Yourself," chap. 3 in *The Discipline of Grace: God's Role and Our Role in the Pursuit of Holiness* (Colorado Springs: NavPress, 1994).

Day 9: The Perfectly Angry Man

1. For a more thorough exploration of righteous anger vs. sinful anger, see Robert D. Jones, "Is Your Anger Really Righteous?" chap. 2 in *Uprooting Anger: Biblical Help for a Common Problem* (Phillipsburg, NJ: P&R Publishing, 2005).

Day 11: Righteous Anger, Augustine, and Your Heart
1. Saint Augustine, *The Confessions of Saint Augustine* (repr., New Kensington, PA: Whitaker House, 1996), 118; emphasis added.
2. Augustine, 118; emphasis added.

Day 13: Why We Get Angry
1. If your preferred English translation uses the word "lusts" or "passions" here, realize that James is not referring to sexual desires per se.

Day 14: What's Wrong with Our Desires?
1. Paul David Tripp, *Instruments in the Redeemer's Hands: People in Need of Change Helping People in Need of Change* (Phillipsburg, NJ: P&R Publishing, 2002), 79.

Day 15: Our Prayers Reveal Our Hearts
1. Alexander Solzhenitsyn, *One Day in the Life of Ivan Denisovich*, trans. Ralph Parker (New York: Penguin, 1963), 154.

Day 16: Playing God
1. I credit "A Biblical View of Anger," ten sermons preached by Gregory C. Nichols at Trinity Baptist Church in Montville, New Jersey, from February to March 1987, for the seeds of this material (although others have made similar observations).

Day 17: God's Grace, Our Hope
1. David Powlison, "Biblical Dynamics of Godly Change" (lecture, Westminster Theological Seminary, Philadelphia, PA, August 1993).

Day 18: The Repentance Prayers of an Angry Couple
1. For this Jack and Jill case study and a fuller version of their prayers, see Robert D. Jones, *Uprooting Anger: Biblical Help for a Common Problem* (Phillipsburg, NJ: P&R Publishing, 2005), 45–47, 73–75.

Day 19: The Spirit, the Flesh, and Revealed Anger
1. See Robert D. Jones, *Uprooting Anger: Biblical Help for a Common Problem* (Phillipsburg, NJ: P&R Publishing, 2005), 78, for a discussion of the various ways we might organize different types of anger.

Day 20: What Revealed Anger Looks Like

1. While the Hebrew text of Proverbs 14:16 lacks an object, several top Proverbs scholars agree that the Lord is in view here, as he is in 1:7; 3:7; 8:13; 9:10; and 14:26–27. See Tremper Longman III, *Proverbs*, Baker Commentary on the Old Testament Wisdom and Psalms (Grand Rapids: Baker Academic, 2006), 301–2; and Bruce K. Waltke, *The Book of Proverbs: Chapters 1–15*, The New International Commentary on the Old Testament (Grand Rapids: Eerdmans, 2004), 595–96.

Day 21: Concealed Anger and Grudge-Bearing

1. See also Robert D. Jones, "Changing Our Angry Behavior: Sinful Concealing," chap. 6 in *Uprooting Anger: Biblical Help for a Common Problem* (Phillipsburg, NJ: P&R Publishing, 2005); and Robert D. Jones, "Battling Bitterness by Grace" and "Redeeming the Art of Rebuke and Granting Forgiveness," chaps. 9 and 10 in *Pursuing Peace: A Christian Guide to Handling Our Conflicts* (Wheaton, IL: Crossway, 2012).

Day 23: Don't Get Mad; Get Patient!

1. Of course, there are times we must confront others (though, even then, we should do so with patience—see 1 Thess. 5:14), but this verse doesn't assume that every offense is one of those times. See Robert D. Jones, *Pursuing Peace: A Christian Guide to Handling Our Conflicts* (Wheaton, IL: Crossway, 2012) for a more thorough discussion on forgiveness (in chap. 8, "To Forgive or Not to Forgive"), including when to confront and when to overlook (in chap. 10, "Redeeming the Art of Rebuke and Granting Forgiveness").

2. Other Proverbs make the same point:

Hatred stirs up conflict,
> but love covers over all wrongs. (Prov. 10:12)

Fools show their annoyance at once,
> but the prudent overlook an insult. (Prov. 12:16)

Whoever would foster love covers over an offense,
but whoever repeats the matter separates close friends.
(Prov. 17:9)

Starting a quarrel is like breaching a dam;
so drop the matter before a dispute breaks out. (Prov.
17:14)

3. Mayo Clinic Staff, "Anger Management: 10 Tips to Tame Your Temper," Mayo Clinic, May 4, 2018, https://www.mayoclinic.org/healthy-lifestyle/adult-health/in-depth/anger-management/art-20045434.

4. "Controlling Anger Before it Controls You," American Psychological Association, accessed September 14, 2018, http://www.apa.org/topics/anger/control.aspx.

5. See *Demolition Man*, directed by Marco Brambilla (1993; Burbank, CA: Warner Bros. Entertainment, 2010), DVD. The phrase also landed in the Urban Dictionary: Urban Dictionary, s.v. "enhance your calm," last modified May 4, 2011, https://www.urbandictionary.com/define.php?term=enhance%20your%20calm.

6. See *Seinfeld*, season 9, episode 3, "The Serenity Now," directed by Andy Ackerman, written by Steve Koren, aired October 9, 1997, on NBC.

7. See *Anger Management*, directed by Peter Segal (2003; Culver City, CA: Columbia TriStar Home Entertainment, 2003), DVD.

Day 26: Don't Get Mad; Get Reconciled!
1. Bible scholars debate whether "against you" is original.

Day 27: Don't Get Mad; Get Content!
1. Jeremiah Burroughs, *The Rare Jewel of Christian Contentment* (1648; repr., Carlisle, PA: Banner of Truth Trust, 1992), 19.

Day 28: Anger at Yourself
1. See Robert D. Jones, "Anger against Yourself," chap. 8 in *Uprooting Anger: Biblical Help for a Common Problem* (Phillipsburg, NJ: P&R Publishing, 2005) for a more thorough discussion of self-anger and for some case study examples.

2. This sometimes leads people to feel a need to "forgive themselves." The dynamics that some call self-forgiveness are closely related to self-anger. See Robert D. Jones, *Forgiveness: "I Just Can't Forgive Myself!"* (Phillipsburg, NJ: P&R Publishing, 2000).

Day 29: Don't Blame God—It's Blasphemy

1. For example, see passages like Genesis 50:20; Psalm 115:3; Lamentations 3:37–38; Daniel 4:35; and Romans 8:28.
2. A careful reading of the story shows that every person in it knew this—Job, Mrs. Job, the servant, God, Satan, and even the writer (who says no more about Satan, in the book's forty-two chapters, after 2:7).
3. As we learned from Jesus in Matt. 12:34; 15:18–20.
4. John Calvin, *Sermons from Job*, ed. and trans. Leroy Nixon (Grand Rapids: Eerdmans, 1952), 29–30.

Day 30: Don't Blame God; Learn to Lament

1. See Robert D. Jones, *Uprooting Anger: Biblical Help for a Common Problem* (Phillipsburg, NJ: P&R Publishing, 2005), 122–25, for biblical examples of lament and for a fuller elaboration of these five components.

Day 31: A Plea to Parents (and All Who Love Children)

1. These verses sync well with other Proverbs that tell us how to differentiate between godly and ungodly friends (see Prov. 1:10; 13:20; 27:5–6).

Conclusion: Where Should You Go Now and Why?

1. For a further unpacking of these reasons, see Robert D. Jones, "Why You Must Deal with Your Sinful Anger," chap. 10 in *Uprooting Anger: Biblical Help for a Common Problem* (Phillipsburg, NJ: P&R Publishing, 2005).

Suggested Resources for the Fight

Books

Jones, Robert D. *Pursuing Peace: A Christian Guide to Handling Our Conflicts*. Wheaton, IL: Crossway, 2012. [A biblical peacemaking manual that parallels more thoroughly some of the themes that are addressed in this book.]

————. *Uprooting Anger: Biblical Help for a Common Problem*. Phillipsburg, NJ: P&R Publishing, 2005. [My first, more comprehensive book on anger, from which I have drawn some material for this devotional book.]

Powlison, David. *Good and Angry: Redeeming Anger, Irritation, Complaining, and Bitterness*. Greensboro, NC: New Growth Press, 2016. [Warm, wise, and pastoral. David was my primary mentor in my doctoral studies on anger. A book that many of us in the biblical counseling world waited long for.]

Welch, Edward T. *A Small Book About a Big Problem: Meditations on Anger, Patience, and Peace*. Greensboro, NC: New Growth Press, 2017. [A brief book that is written in a topical, fifty-day devotional format, from another of my doctoral professors.]

Booklets

Emlet, Michael R. *Angry Children: Understanding and Helping Your Child Regain Control*. Greensboro, NC: New Growth Press, 2008. [Due to space limits and my adult-reader focus, I didn't address anger in children in this book. Mike's booklet would be a good starting place.]

Jones, Robert D. *Angry at God? Bring Him Your Doubts and Questions*. Phillipsburg, NJ: P&R Publishing, 2003. [A stand-alone booklet that was revised and included as chapter 6 in my *Uprooting Anger* book.]

————. *Freedom from Resentment: Stopping Hurts from Turning Bitter*. Greensboro, NC: New Growth Press, 2010. [A stand-alone booklet that was revised and included as chapter 6 in my *Pursuing Peace* book. Provides six explicitly gospel-centered truths that fight against resentment and bitterness.]

———. *When Trouble Shows Up: Seeing God's Transforming Love.* Greensboro, NC: New Growth Press, 2013. [Presents seven specific ways that God uses hardships to make us more like Christ. Useful in the "put on" replacement process of fighting against anger.]

BIBLICAL COUNSELING COALITION

The Biblical Counseling Coalition (BCC) is passionate about enhancing and advancing biblical counseling globally. We accomplish this through broadcasting, connecting, and collaborating.

Broadcasting promotes gospel-centered biblical counseling ministries and resources to bring hope and healing to hurting people around the world. We promote biblical counseling in a number of ways: through our *15:14* podcast, website (biblicalcounselingcoalition.org), partner ministry, conference attendance, and personal relationships.

Connecting biblical counselors and biblical counseling ministries is a central component of the BCC. The BCC was founded by leaders in the biblical counseling movement who saw the need for and the power behind building a strong global network of biblical counselors. We introduce individuals and ministries to one another to establish gospel-centered relationships.

Collaboration is the natural outgrowth of our connecting efforts. We truly believe that biblical counselors and ministries can accomplish more by working together. The BCC Confessional Statement, which is a clear and comprehensive definition of biblical counseling, was created through the cooperative effort of over thirty leading biblical counselors. The BCC has also published a three-part series of multi-contributor works that bring theological wisdom and practical expertise to pastors, church leaders, counseling practitioners, and students. Each year we are able to facilitate the production of numerous resources, including books, articles, videos, audio resources, and a host of other helps for biblical counselors. Working together allows us to provide robust resources and develop best practices in biblical counseling so that we can hone the ministry of soul care in the church.

To learn more about the BCC, visit biblicalcounselingcoalition.org.

Was this book helpful to you?
Consider writing a review online.
The author appreciates your feedback!

Or write to P&R at editorial@prpbooks.com
with your comments. We'd love to hear from you.